CORAZÓN PURO

CORAZÓN PURO

A Memoir of Ministry

CURRIE BURRIS

RESOURCE *Publications* • Eugene, Oregon

CORAZÓN PURO
A Memoir of Ministry

Resource Publications
An Imprint of Wipf and Stock Publishers
199 W. 8th Ave., Suite 3
Eugene, OR 97401

www.wipfandstock.com

PAPERBACK ISBN: 978–1-6667–3566–6
HARDCOVER ISBN: 978–1-6667–9298–0
EBOOK ISBN: 978–1-6667–9299–7

JANUARY 7, 2022 11:30 AM

Grateful acknowledgement is made to the following for permission to
reprint from previously published material:

Lucy Atkinson Rose, excerpt from *Songs in the Night: A Witness to God's
Love in Life and in Death*. Copyright@1998 by Ben Lacy Rose. CTS Press,
Decatur, Georgia.

Currie Burris, excerpt from *Speak Lord, I'm Listening: Devotional Messages
to help you hear God speaking to you in the Scriptures*. Copyright@1999 by
Ben L. Rose.

Dedicated to Marsha Stalcup,
the love of my life

Have mercy on me, O God,
according to your steadfast love;
according to your abundant mercy
blot out my transgressions.
Wash me thoroughly from my iniquity,
and cleanse me from my sin.

For I know my transgressions,
and my sin is ever before me.
Against you, you alone, have I sinned,
and done what is evil in your sight,
so that you are justified in your sentence
and blameless when you pass judgment.
Indeed, I was born guilty,
a sinner when my mother conceived me.

You desire truth in the inward being;
Therefore, teach me wisdom in my secret heart.
Purge me with hyssop, and I shall be clean;
wash me, and I shall be whiter than snow.
Let me hear joy and gladness;
let the bones that you have crushed rejoice.
Hide your face from my sins,
and blot out all my iniquities.

Create in me a clean heart, O God,
and put a new and right spirit within me.
Do not cast me away from your presence,
and do not take your holy spirit from me.
Restore to me the joy of your salvation,
and sustain in me a willing spirit.

(PSALM 51: 1–12 NRSV)

CONTENTS

ACKNOWLEDGEMENTS

I ESPECIALLY WISH TO THANK my family, friends and mentors who have filled the course and direction of this life in ministry. Particularly I wish to thank my wife, Marsha Stalcup, who is my companion and partner in every phase of my ministry. She is the love of my life. In many ways, her love saved my life and filled every day with joy and hope. I want to thank my daughters, Hannah Guzewicz and Rachel Mullins, whose births were the miracles that enveloped my life. My sisters, Ginger Burris and Candice Burcher, shared the joy and the sorrow of my family stories. I love them dearly.

I want to acknowledge my teachers and mentors who shaped my theological vision and guided my path in ministry: Elie Wiesel, Pierre Teilhard de Chardin, Dorothy Day, Thomas Merton, Meister Eckhardt, Richard Rubenstein, Thomas J.J. Altizer, and Joe Coppage.

I send much love and appreciation to the members and friends of the two congregations that I served, Clifton Presbyterian Church and Silver Spring Presbyterian Church. Your love and support created the new community of grace that filled my ministry.

I thank God for the companionship and guidance of my colleagues and friends in ministry through the many miles and many years: James Manley, Charles Swain, John Collins, David Smedley, Rex Kaney, Lucy Rose, Nyansako Ni Nku, Justin Njikue, Timothy Njoya, Bill Teng, Ed Taylor, and my longtime friends, Michael Boon and Roy Howard.

1

A PILGRIMAGE

IN THE BEGINNING OF 2020, Marsha and I started out on a road trip, a cross country journey by car across the United States. We began our trip in our home in Maryland and traveled by interstate across the central cross-country route through the mid-west, the central plains of Oklahoma and Texas, the high deserts of New Mexico and Arizona, over the High Sierras and into the central valley of California. The trip was really a pilgrimage of sorts, a spiritual journey to visit the oldest member of our family, Marsha's mother, Jean Tauber, and then welcome the birth of the newest member of the family, Samuel Guzewicz.

This pilgrimage included visits to multiple National Parks and Monuments along the way. On display was the incredible beauty and wonder of the national world: Hot Springs National Park, Petroglyphs National Monument, the Petrified Forest National Park, Meteor Crater Park, the Mojave Desert, Sequoia and King's Canyon National Park.

We arrived in Visalia, California just a few days before the arrival of the most incredible natural wonder ever witnessed, the birth of our grandson. Hannah, our daughter, had gone into labor earlier than expected. She went to the hospital with her husband, Tim, and her mid-wife mother, Marsha. I stayed at home with the two older sisters, Eleanor and Penny. Sammy was born in the early hours of the morning, assisted by a midwife and caught by his grandmother. I brought the girls to the hospital a few hours later to meet their new brother. We all laughed and cried with the sight of this life, born joyfully into the world, surrounded by his loving family.

I took Sammy into my arms, wrapped him in a warm blanket, and raised him high into the sky. I prayed a prayer of welcome. I prayed a prayer of blessing. I touched his head with a seal of flowing water, and graced his brow with a holy kiss. The miracle of new life. A blessed child of God.

After Sammy came home from the hospital and everyone had time to rest and settle into the shape of a new, gathered family, we began to prepare for return trip across the country. We visited more parks and monuments, Death Valley National Park and Yosemite National Park. Both were breathtaking and beautiful. Yosemite was full of soaring majesty. Death Valley was endless shimmering flats of salt and sand ringed by rugged rough textured rocky, mountains, watched over by blazing winter sun.

On our return trip we again passed through the Mojave Desert, and then dropped down to the border regions of Arizona and New Mexico. We drove through Organ Pipe Cactus National Monument, and touched the notorious border wall between Mexico and the US. We hiked through some of the Saguaro National Park and struck out through White Sands National Park. We went underground in the Carlsbad Caverns National Park and then drove across the whole state of Texas in one day. The last park on our journey was the smallest, Little River National Park in Alabama. It is just a thin strip of a park along the Alabama Georgia border, but very striking in power and movement.

We arrived back home literally days before the international pandemic was declared and all travel and social gathering was shut down. Curfews, quarantines and shutdowns began in mid-March, and by the end of the month, life had changed forever. From that time on, we would mark our lives by life before, and life after the pandemic. Schools were closed, church services stopped. Only essential businesses remained open. No restaurants, bars or social gatherings. Everyone had to wear masks in public, methodically wash hands and surfaces, and strictly keep social distance everywhere.

The first death by the Coronavirus pandemic in the United States was reported in February 29th, although it was learned later that the first deaths probably happened months before. The number dying only grew and skyrocketed into April and May. Death was everywhere. No one was safe or immune. Any social contact or interaction could become a source of infection and potentially death. What had always before been the very definition of life, rich and full, life together with other people, could now portend the exact opposite.

Through the Spring of the year, the death toll rose to astronomical numbers. Worldwide over 200,000 dead, millions infected, every country in the world affected by the pandemic. By the summer however, the first wave of the pandemic had crested. Numbers were beginning to fall. Businesses, schools and churches were beginning to figure out ways to operate again, if only by distances, remotely and online.

The YMCA where Marsha and I are members figured out it could reopen in July in a very restricted and social distanced way. The pool would be open for swimming for members by appointment only, very limited numbers and limited time slots. So we reserved lanes for lap swimming, two to three times a week throughout the summer. We began swimming on a regular basis for the first time in July and every week thereafter. In a world surrounded by the pandemic, swimming the lanes in heat of the afternoon sun became a rejuvenating, lifegiving moment.

Since I retired in 2018, after 40 years of ordained ministry in the peace and social justice movement, on the national staff of the Presbyterian Church, and in two local congregations, I had committed to writing a memoir, a reflection of the meaning and direction of all those years of service in the church. I began by gathering stories and events that had been a part of that life and ministry. I collected stories I had used as sermon illustrations, stories that had been a part of my various degree programs and stories I had never written down or told to anyone ever in my life.

But by the summer of 2020, those stories were just fragments, fleeting memories of a life lived. They were only stories without any connecting tissue, without any purpose or direction. I still could not find the revealed meaning of my ministry. That is, until I began to swim. Each day in the pool I would swim laps, up and back in the pool on my back, doing variations of a back stroke so I could swim while looking up into the blue summer sky. Water, sky, wispy clouds floating by as I rhythmically made my way back and forth.

I began to think about my life. I recalled all those stories I was collecting. I rehearsed them again and again, filling in the beginnings and endings, connecting the different stages and phases of my life. And all the while I kept asking the same questions. Why did this happen? What was the real purpose of this decision?

I remembered the seven-year-old boy who rose up from the pew during the altar call of a revival service of my Baptist church to walk down to the front of the church to commit my life to God for the first time.

I thought about the seventeen-year-old who refused to go on the church youth group retreat to an amusement park in central Florida because the venture was not serious enough, not focused on growing spiritually.

I thought about sticking my thumb out at the on-ramp of the Florida turnpike the spring of my sophomore year in college to hitchhike across the United States and Canada.

I thought of standing vigil at the hospital bed side of my fatally injured grandmother, suffering for almost a month.

I thought of marching in the streets of New York City for a Nuclear Weapon Freeze before greeting a million people rallied in Central Park.

I thought of standing vigil outside the Georgia prison for the execution of Roosevelt Green.

I thought of preaching my first sermon at Clifton Presbyterian Church, a church in a shelter for homeless men.

I remembered baptizing in their hospital incubator two twin infants, born prematurely just days before they both died less than a month old.

I remembered praying by the bedside of a seminary professor as she succumbed to cancer with the words of the doxology on her lips.

I remembered preaching to a congregation of five thousand gathered in an open field in Buea, Cameroon on the occasion of the fiftieth anniversary of the Christian Women Fellowship of the Presbyterian Church of Cameroon.

I remembered praying by the lifeless body of my grandson as he lay in repose after dying from a sudden fever at the age of ten months.

I remembered dancing with the whole congregation at my final service at Silver Spring Presbyterian Church, singing together the chorus, "Bend low, bend low, and see what the Lord will do!"

It's then that I realized what it all had been about. I understood the real calling and purpose of my ministry. I realized that it had begun long before I was ever ordained. I understood that it involved my whole life, not just what I did in the life of the church. And I awakened to true purpose and reason for my ministry. It was not as I had imagined on the first night walking across the seminary campus in Louisville in 1976, but it was as revealed to me on the very last night of my ministry, a night of fear and trembling at a casa, Corazon Puro, the first stop on the Camino de Santiago in Spain in 2015. Beginnings and endings. Life and death.

2

BECOMING

"For God so loved the world that he gave his only Son, so that everyone who believes in him may not perish but may have eternal life."

(JOHN 3:16 NRSV)

I SAT ALONE, by myself on the back pew of the large sanctuary of
the First Baptist Church of Ft. Lauderdale. It was the first night
of a five-day series of revival services. Each night, the faithful
would gather in the church for singing, prayers and preaching.
The hymns were the traditional gospel hymns of faith and salvation, "Just as I Am" or "I Surrender all." The prayers were long and
fervent, prayers for the lost souls of everyone gathered there.

The sermons always concluded with an "altar call," a sum-
moning of anyone there to make their personal profession of faith
in Jesus Christ as their Lord and Savior. As the preacher prayed,
with every head bowed and every eye closed, people were invited
to stand and walk down to the front of the church. There each one
confessed their sins before God, and surrendered their life into the
grace and mercy of Jesus Christ.

That night in the revival meeting, I was seven years old. I always remembered that night as a turning point in my life. It was the first reference point for all the changes that would shape me for the rest of my life. But interestingly for the longest time I didn't realize I was so young when it happened. Some forty-five years later I went back to First Baptist Church in Ft. Lauderdale and asked for my baptismal record. And they produced the proof that I was barely in second grade at the time. How could someone so young understand what was being asked by the preacher that night? How could I stand alone and walk that aisle at just seven?

I was totally shaken and moved by the call of the preacher. In tears, I stood, and without prodding or pressure from anyone, not my parents or my friends, I walked down the long aisle of the church and accepted God into my life. I took the preacher's hand and, along with the dozen others or so who had likewise marched down the aisle, we prayed and gave our hearts to Jesus.

That moment was a spiritual awakening for me. It was like waking up for the first time to realize that I was not then and had never been alone. God in Jesus Christ was with me from the moment I was born, was fully there beside me in the front of that church that night, and would be there before me, behind me, above me and within me forever.

I didn't fully understand that at first. In fact, I have spent the rest of my life trying to understand the fully meaning and purpose of that walk down the aisle that night. I have struggled to understand what kind of transformation occurred that night. How had my life changed by surrendering my will and fate into the hands of God? What was the nature of this new relationship that was to shape everything that I was then and everything I would become? And most importantly, how could I understand the presence and power of God in my life in the times when I felt no presence of God at all? How could I hold the love of God in my heart when I felt no love of God at all, when all I felt in life was sorrow, bitterness and death?

Since that night of conversion in the church revival, my journey in the heart of God has been filled with wonder, joy, love and excitement, and with struggle, questioning, doubt, anger and fear. There have been times of ecstatic transport, or lustrous epiphany, carried away with the shining presence of divine holiness. And there have been moments of anguish and loss, grinding emptiness and alienation. Life with God has been anything but easy. Perhaps it is because life with God has always been shaped by life and death, joy and sorrow, love and madness, fullness and loss. Somehow God is in both these poles of existence. And figuring out how to be in both is the substance of the journey.

Come Follow Me

> As Jesus passed along the Sea of Galilee, he saw Simon and his brother Andrew casting a net into the sea—for they were fishermen. [17] And Jesus said to them, "Follow me and I will make you fish for people." [18] And immediately they left their nets and followed him. [19] As he went a little farther, he saw James, son of Zebedee and his brother John, who were in their boat mending the nets. [20] Immediately he called them; and they left their father Zebedee in the boat with the hired men, and followed him. (Mark 1:16–20, NRSV)

When I was a young boy, our family lived in a suburban community with lots of other families with kids our age. It was, as we perceived it, a safe community. We didn't worry about crime or the dangers that we often associate with living in communities these days. It was safe for a young kid like me to go outside in the afternoons after school and just play. We would run from yard to yard, block to block, playing games, riding our bikes, exploring the lake and canals near our home.

There were no fences separating one person's property from another, no limits to how far we could roam—except that we could go no further than the sound of my mother's voice would carry. Because at the end of the day, when the sun was going down and she had finished preparing dinner and set the table, my mother would step out the front door and call us home. Each one of my sisters and me, she would call out our names.

Other parents might be doing the same thing, calling their children, but when we heard our names—when I heard my name—I knew it was time for me to come home. "Currie, Currie" and I knew it was time to stop the game, stop the exploring, stop wherever I was, whatever I was doing and go home. When I heard my name, it was time to go home.

This was the same calling that I heard in my heart every day, every hour since I first walked down the aisle at the revival meeting when I was seven years old. It was the calling I heard every Sunday in worship, singing the songs of faith, praying the prayers of commitment. The same calling I heard at school, in classrooms, playing games with my friends, playing football and baseball, working in the yard with my father, shopping or cooking with my mother, praying prayers at the dinner table, or praying prayers of blessing at night before bed. The same calling to come home, come home to God.

Craven Cullum Burris

My grandfather, my father's father, was Craven Cullom Burris. But he was rarely ever called by his full name. He was always "C.C. Burris." His friends, his family, his colleagues at the college where he taught, the parishioners at the churches where he preached, all called him C.C. Burris. In fact, the name "C.C." became somewhat of a family tradition. Each generation that followed him found a way to name one of their offspring some combination of names that resulted in another "C.C." in the family. I have one cousin named "Christa Cullom" called "CeCe." Another named 'Christopher Cullom," and a nephew called "Christopher Currie." My own grandson was named "Charles Currie" also called "C.C."

My father's mother, grandmother Burris, was Virginia Currie Burris. She was originally from eastern North Carolina from Scottish heritage. I claim linkage to Scotland from her. Her family, the "Currie's", were Scots presbyterian and although she married a

Baptist minister, she never let it be forgotten where her roots were. She was a strikingly beautiful woman, long straight hair, always drawn up into a bun. One of my most vivid memory of her is in the evening near bedtime as she released the pins and brushed her long silvery grey hair, gently lovingly.

I remember my grandfather as a kind and gentle man. He was rather frail, older looking than his years, thin, wisps of white hair across his bald scalp. He was always too weak to play with us his grandchildren. But we could sit in his lap as he told us stories and sang little songs. He loved to sing "Danny Boy" though I'm not sure he always sang all the words or even finished a full verse.

My grandfather was a Baptist minister. He preached in a number of small churches of rural North Carolina, sometimes serving several congregations at the same time, something like a circuit rider. Several of his churches were called "mission" churches, churches in formation, on their way to becoming independent congregations on their own. He was also a teacher and professor at Wingate College, a small school in Union County, North Carolina.

Dr. Burris was also a scholar. He loved literature, the classics of Greece and Rome, as well Shakespeare and Milton. It was very common for his sermons to be sprinkled with quotes from Aristotle or Virgil, from Macbeth or A Pilgrim's Progress, as much as from the Gospels or the Psalms. He was called "Dr." Burris as an honorary title, as he never completed a Ph.D. But it was also because he was dearly loved, by all his students and colleagues alike.

He became President of Wingate College in the late 1920's just in time to become the steward of the institution through the dark years of the Depression. Somehow, he was able to keep the school afloat in the years when no one was able to afford much in tuition and he was paid by barter in-kind as much as actual salary. The school flourished in those years, grew in student body, and became a full, four-year institution under his watch.

I didn't realize it at the time--the time that I knew and loved my grandfather, the time that I watched him as preacher and pastor of small country churches, the time that I observed him as teacher and professor, leading in faith and knowledge--I didn't realize that he would be my first role model as a minister. C.C. Burris was the kind of pastor I always wanted to be: prophetic, intelligent, lyrical, kind, compassionate and loving. I wanted to be like my grandfather.

In January of my senior year of high school we received the call that notified us that my grandfather had died. He had always presented as physically weak and somewhat frail. He had what was always called "a heart condition." That year he passed away shortly after suffering a heart attack. His heart just stopped. Our family journeyed back to North Carolina for the funeral. We arrived in Wingate, his home town, in time for the viewing of the body in the funeral home.

More than anything else that happened around his passing, more than the receiving the news, more than the long trip back home, more than funeral service itself or the grave side interment, I remember standing beside his open casket, looking at his lifeless gray skin, his empty face, wisps of white hair drawn across his scalp. I remember this, the first dead body I had ever seen, and I remember wordlessly praying for my grandfather in the presence of death.

Some fifty-two years later, in 2021, as I am writing the words of this reflection on my ministry, I realize that standing vigil next to the body of my grandfather, C.C. Burris, was the first real act of ministry in my life. It was the first time I would give witness to the reality of suffering and heartbreaking truth of death. It was the first time I would hold the ultimate pain and finality of life before the ultimate love and suffering of God.

3

PREPARATION

AT FLORIDA STATE UNIVERSITY, I was a religion major and philosophy minor. There was never any doubt about it after I took my first religion class under an extraordinary professor, Charles Swain. He opened up the study of religion, not just as an academic pursuit, but as a spiritual quest, a search across the history of religions and the broad and deep scope of theological diversity. He opened up for me the search for God, the deep longing for unity with the "ground of all being."

From the beginning, I was fascinated by the mystical tradition. I studied the search for union with the divine in the multitude of expressions in Hinduism, the teachers of enlightenment like Jiddu Krishnamurti and Paramahamsa Yogananda. I studied the expressions of mysticism in native American spiritual teachers like Carlos Castaneda. I dived deep into the Taoist tradition and Buddhism, particularly Mahayana and Zen Buddhism. I began to practice various forms of meditation from the Yoga and Zen practice.

Paradoxically, it was through the study of Zen that I discovered the writings of Thomas Merton, the Christian Trappist monk. Merton's book, "Mystics and Zen Masters" opened to me the world of Christian mysticism, and in a way, brought me back home to the tradition I was born into. I discovered St. John of the

Cross, the Pseudo-Dionysius, St. Francis of Assisi, and the Cloud of Unknowing. I did an extended independent study of the work of Meister Eckhardt, captivated by his notion of the "Eternal now" and the real nature of time. I did an honors thesis on Teresa of Avila's "Interior Castle," claiming her vision of the unity in ecstasy with God.

But it was Merton's own work that ultimately became my primary teacher. I read everything he every wrote. I immersed myself in his spiritual quest. His powerful short book, "Bread in the Wilderness" became my personal bible, sustenance in a lonely spiritual sojourn. I ultimately made a pilgrimage to his monastery in Kentucky, Gethsemane, to visit his grave and to pray in the woods where he lived in hermitage.

My spiritual practice became quite focused. I studied meditation and I practiced various forms of meditation. I used Hindu chant, Zen silence, native American drumming, self-hypnosis, and Christian Centering prayer. I sought obliteration of the ego, silence of the voices in my head, submergence into the Dharma, suspension of time, and ecstatic union with the divine.

But one experience changed all of my study and changed my practice forever thereafter. I came in from class one cool, fall afternoon and lay on my bed to begin to practice of some things I had been learning. I lay on my bed, closed my eyes, began calming and centering my breathing. I slowly began counting my breaths and chanting my chosen spirit word, "Abba-Amma" and Aramaic form of father-mother. Slowly, slowly, the pressures and stresses of the day began to slip away. I consciously began relaxing all the muscles in my body, on-by-one, starting with my toes, my feet, my ankles, calves, thighs, and on and on up until I was relaxing and releasing each muscle in my face, mouth, scalp and eyes. My whole body felt numb.

My consciousness became detached from my body; I began to float just above my body. Just an inch or so at first, but I could clearly perceive that my mind was beginning to hover in the room. Though my eyes were closed, I could see the walls, the ceiling and doors, I turned to look out the window. I turned over a little further, enough to roll and look down at my body. I was floating near the top of the room.

Then, with a kind of swoosh, without a thought, a direction or intention, I was outside and above the house, rising higher and higher. I rose above the whole neighborhood. I could see everything. I'm not sure how long this lasted. Was it a second, a minute, an hour? But as quickly as this out-of-the body experience occurred, I was overcome with a powerful feeling of fear and panic. What should have been blissful, became terrifying. I was afraid that I would be lost forever, afraid that I could never get back to my body. And so, just as quickly, it was all over. I was back on my bed, back in my body, eyes blinking open. My body still felt paralyzed; I could not move at first, until I willed each muscle to operate again. Slowly I was back.

I have never had this experience again. I am not sure I ever wanted to have this experience again. I continued in my spiritual practice. I continued to use Christian Centering prayer. I even used to teach Centering Prayer in my work as a spiritual Director. But I never truly sought that ecstatic experience again. If this was union with God, then I was too afraid to seek it again.

It was many years later, almost forty-five years later to be more exact, that I experienced complete union with God once again. It wasn't in spiritual ecstasy. It wasn't the fruit of torturous meditation discipline. It wasn't out of any intentionality at all. I was simply driving though a neighborhood on my way to an appointment with my spiritual director. For months I had been meeting with my director struggling with my crushing grief and spiritual crisis in the aftermath of the death of my grandson. I was driving to see her again, searching for something to report to her, something to offer as a sign of my healing and renewal, when my eyes just opened.

Quietly and peacefully, I awakened to an undeniable awareness that God was right there with me. In the ordinariness of simply living life, God was before me, behind me, above me below me, completely through me. I was immersed in God right then and there, and in truth I had always been so. I had been bathed in an ecstatic union with God from the first breath of my birth, every moment of every day, and I would always be so. I didn't have to search for it, didn't have to struggle for it, didn't have to earn it or achieve. It would never leave me no matter often I ignore it or deny it. I didn't have to be afraid of it either, although in that moment and in those days of suffering and grief, I was paralyzed in fear. The presence of God terrorized me. I pray that it will not always be so.

A Dwelling Place

When I was nineteen years old, half-way through my sophomore year at college, I quit. I dropped out. It was only briefly as it turned out, but at that point I decided not to enroll in the spring semester and I wasn't sure I was coming back. I'm not exactly sure why I did it—restlessness, longing for adventure, searching for something I wasn't finding in school. I packed up my backpack with a sleeping bag, a change of clothes, a book or two, two hundred dollars in my pocket, and I headed out to the Florida Turnpike and stuck out my thumb. I didn't know where I was going, just headed north, or even where I would be spending the night that night.

I spent the next five months hitch hiking around the US and Canada, sometimes by myself and sometimes with my friend, Michael Boon. Up and down the east coast, across the Trans-Canadian highway, down to California for a month at Berkeley, then back across the US--Nevada, Utah, Nebraska, Iowa, and the mid-west .

But I still remember the look on my mother and father's faces when I told them what I was going to do. Fear, panic, worry, searching for something to say that would stop me from embarking on this crazy scheme, at the same time knowing that there was probably nothing they could say that would stop me. I can't imagine what my mother felt as she left me at the on-ramp to the expressway.

I remember getting into a car in northern Virginia, following the interstate across the Potomac River and seeing the cityscape of Washington DC for the first time—the Jefferson Memorial, the

Washington Monument, the green stretches of the Mall, the White House and then the Capitol.

I remember riding into New York City, through the Holland Tunnel, navigating the streets of Manhattan, seeing the World Trade Center towers, the Empire State Building, Central Park, sleeping in a friend's dorm room at Columbia University, and hearing Jiddu Krishnamurti speak at Carnegie Hall. I remember hearing the "Who's Next" album for the first time in a dorm room at Harvard University in Cambridge, Massachusetts, hitching up the pike up into New Hampshire, across Franconia notch, discovering granola at Franconia College, and then thumbing back down again to Portland, Maine.

A few weeks later I showed up at my grandparent's home in North Carolina, stayed a few days. They had the same fear and worry as I left them. They offered me anything if I would just get on a bus and go home.

A few weeks later, I left on a second hitching trip, this time with my good friend, Michael Boon. We hiked up the east coast again and then up into Canada. We slept on a hostel room floor in Montreal and headed out across the Trans-Canadian Highway. We slept in the back of van and sometimes along the side of the highway. One day we stood for eighteen hours at a truck stop outside the tiny town called "Wawa" on the northern shore of Lake Superior. We finally got a ride after begging a travelling hippie to take us to the next town after he stopped at the gas station.

We then made our way across the broad, unending plains of southern Canada. For many days it was flat fields of grain and open country, until we reached western Alberta and the Rocky Mountains rose in the distance. At an RV campsite in Calgary, Alberta, I called my parents, collect from pay phone. They offered to send me money for a plane ticket, if I would just come home. But I continued on. We began the slow winding trek up the mountainsides, higher and higher.

Finally, we made our way up past the tree line, high mountain lakes, and then past frozen ice sheet glaciers. At the top of Glacier National Park, we stopped near the summit of Mt. Dawson.

We could see for hundreds of miles in all directions, innumerable mountain peaks, snows and glaciers, the Canadian plains far off to the east and the mist of pacific to the west. We stood gazing across the infinite vista for a timeless moment. Awesome beauty, wonder, and grace.

I beheld the glory of God's creation, shining brightly. I saw the glory of God's creation, as it has always been. I felt the presence of God.

We finally got to California a week later, and hung out a while in UC Berkeley campus. I hitched down the valley to Monterey, nodded at Esalen Institute passing by, and hiked up into the mountains behind Big Sur. There on the mountaintop, I found another shining moment of vision and insight. A few seeks later, we got a ride all the way across the country through Nevada, Utah, and Colorado. In a small valley outside Colorado Springs, we took a small dirt road up into the hills and found a hot spring cascading down the mountainside, merging into a cool mountain stream. There, the hot water was segregated by rocks into pools of different temps. We skinny–dipped in the pools along with dozens of other transient hippies who had likewise found this hidden natural gem.

We made our way across Nebraska, stopping at a notorious strip of wild hemp bushes growing along the side of the road. We packed several garbage bags full of the harvested wild growth and stowed them in the trunk of our car, travelling the rest of our journey paranoid about the possibility of getting stopped by the police with the illegal weed in our trunk. We parted ways with the college ride share driver in Kentucky and then hitched back south, arriving back at Florida State University in Tallahassee to enroll for the fall semester.

All the while on this trip I was convinced I was completely safe. A lot of young people my age were doing the same thing. We had not yet heard about the murderers and rapists who preyed on unsuspecting hitchhikers. The dangers were there, we just had not heard of them yet. And surely today I would never do anything like that again. Nor would I recommend it for anyone else.

But my parents didn't want me to stop growing, stop learning, or to exploring myself or the world. They loved me and they just wanted me to be safe.

Riding on the Storm

[22] Immediately Jesus made the disciples get into the boat and go on ahead of him to the other side, while he dismissed the crowd. [23] After he had dismissed them, he went up on a mountainside by himself to pray. Later that night, he was there alone, [24] and the boat was already a considerable distance from land, buffeted by the waves because the wind was against it.

[25] Shortly before dawn Jesus went out to them, walking on the lake. [26] When the disciples saw him walking on the lake, they were terrified. "It's a ghost," they said, and cried out in fear.

[27] But Jesus immediately said to them: "Take courage! It is I. Don't be afraid."

[28] "Lord, if it's you," Peter replied, "tell me to come to you on the water."

[29] "Come," he said.

Then Peter got down out of the boat, walked on the water and came toward Jesus. [30] But when he saw the wind, he was afraid and, beginning to sink, cried out, "Lord, save me!"

[31] Immediately Jesus reached out his hand and caught him. "You of little faith," he said, "why did you doubt?"

[32] And when they climbed into the boat, the wind died down. [33] Then those who were in the boat worshiped him, saying, "Truly you are the Son of God."

(Matthew 14:22–33, NRSV)

Forty years ago, I was just out of college and had no idea of what I wanted to do with my life. That year, I took numerous jobs. I drove a taxi on the streets of Tallahassee, carrying ordinary and some famous people back and forth around town. One day took

Sly Stone (of Sly and the Family Stone) and his entourage to the airport after one of his concerts.

One day, while I was still in Tallahassee, I saw an ad in the paper: "Wanted: commercial fishermen, no experience necessary." Sounded interesting to me, although I had no idea what I was getting into. I called the number in the ad and was given a time and a ship to report to at the docks of Carrabelle, a small town just south of Tallahassee on the coast of the Gulf of Mexico. I screwed up my courage and drove down.

I arrived the night before we were to leave. After searching about a bit, I found the captain in a bar near the docks. He sent me back to the boat to find a bunk and said we would talk in the morning. The room was small and cramped, smelled of fish and burned fuel oil. I remember crawling into that bunk thinking I should leave, right then. Run now while no one was looking. But I stayed there, hunkered down and waited.

In the light of the morning, I realized that the boat I was going out on was small, no more that 40 feet. I met the rest of the crew, just four of us all together, three plus the captain. One was an old man who had been a fisherman all his life. White hair and sea worn, he showed me around, showed me most of what I needed to know: how to cut bait, bait the hooks (ten hooks on a six-foot leader line) and then how to lower the line from the large reel (no rod, just a reel about 12 inches in diameter holding about 200 feet of line). A three-pound weight would carry the line to the bottom. You place your fingers on the line and felt a bump on the line as a fish would take the bait from each hook. When you felt about ten bumps, you start reeling in the line.

The other member of the crew, like myself, had never done any commercial fishing before. He was in his forties and had just married a young woman. She didn't look older than 18, but they had nothing, only the clothes in their suitcase. He left her on the dock with $10 and a paid-up room in a cheap motel. We left Carrabelle for 10 days on the Gulf of Mexico.

The captain was tall and thin, in his forties, streaks of grey in his hair. He wore blue jeans and a tee shirt, barefoot. He had only one arm. He told me he lost his right arm in a mill accident when he was a boy. I particularly remember the tee shirt he wore the whole trip, a white tee shirt with the Newport cigarette slogan emblazoned across the front: "Alive with pleasure." With his one and a half arms he could bait and drop more line, reel in more fish than the all the rest of us.

He also had been on the sea most of his life. He owned three fishing boats, one like this one that was going out at the same time with us but would separate and fish another part of the Gulf. The third boat was being worked on the repair shop. The captain had borrowed the money to buy these boats from the man who owned the fish processing plant, the only fish processing plant in Carrabelle.

This fish man would buy all our catch from us when we returned. The captain also owed the fish man for all our food for the ten days on the sea, all of our fuel oil for the boats, our bait, and the ice to pack the fish in we caught. The income from the sale of our fish was intended to pay all the expenses all the captains boats.

Before we left sight of land, I began to get seasick. The small boat was bucking up and down on the gulf waves and I was green. It was too late to turn back, too much was riding on this trip. We needed every daylight hour to fish. So, for three days I couldn't hold anything down. But I could not stop to lie down. I would fish all day, throw up between drops of the lines and go back to fishing.

The first day we went about 50 miles out into the gulf, into deep water about 200 feet deep. We fished all day, using sonar to find schools of fish near the ocean floor. Dropped our lines at each school. Usually, we would pull up a mix of large 20-to-30-pound grouper and 10-to-15-pound snapper with each drop. As you quickly pull the leader full of fish onto the deck of the boat, you take six, seven, eight fish off your line each time, then bait up the hooks again as fast as you can, and drop the line again. Before the day is over the deck is covered with fish, some places are knee-deep in fish.

The captain kept a large percolator of coffee brewing in the galley all day long, add more grounds to the old throughout the day. He usually would put a pot of dried lima beans on the stove in the morning, which would cook all day to be ready for dinner that night. At the end of the day when the sun started to set, the captain would start fixing dinner. He would choose one the grouper on the deck, scale it, gut it, cut it up and fry it. Fried fish and lima beans, eaten from the bow of a rolling ship, far out in the gulf, never tasted so good.

While he was cooking, the rest of the crew would start gutting the day's catch, throwing the fish entrails over board. I clearly remember reaching inside the cavity of each fish, grabbing the guts and pulling them out. Often my fingers would wrap around the still-beating heart of the dying fish. From there we would pack all the day's catch in ice in the belly of the boat.

Bedtime was after dinner when the sun went down. Each of us would have to take a three-hour watch during the night while the others slept. It was those long hours in the middle of the night that I remember the most. Alone on a small craft a hundred miles from the shore, the stars never shone brighter. The sea never seemed so huge, so dangerous, so much like an infinite undulating mother, threatening, undefinable, and yet comforting.

I brought a book to read during the down times between fishing runs. It was *Autobiography of a Yogi* by Paramahamsa Yogananda. I was a religion major at Florida State University with a major emphasis on eastern and western mysticism. Yogananda was a prominent spiritual master in eastern mysticism of the early 20th century. He taught the unity of the original spirituality of Jesus Christ and Hindu philosophy. He taught a type of meditation practice that led to spiritual union with God, advanced levels of consciousness and mystical ecstatic visions and experiences. He told stories of mystical experiences, visions of past spiritual masters, physical levitation, out the body experiences, and complete union with the divine being.

As I rode the waves of an infinite ocean, I breathed deep the salt spray and burned in the intensity of all-day sun. As I repetitively dropped my heavy line laden with bait to the bottom of the sea and pulled back fish after fish, again and again for hours at a time, at the same time I removed each fish from the hook and flung them on the deck. As I slit the belly of each fish, removed the guts, I packed them on ice and return to bait the hooks for another run. As I repetitively immersed myself in the same tasks, over and over again, hour after hour, day after day, I found myself slipping into the same kind of meditation that Yogananda embodied. I found the line between self and the ego begin to slip away. I found the bounds of past, present and future begin to blur. I found a hazy, tentative, unsure spiritual union begin to touch edges of my spirit. Just a touch, just a taste, but with a longing for more.

On the fifth day out, we were some 200 miles out into the Gulf. I had the fourth watch, three to six in the morning. A storm blew up from out of nowhere. It started with rain, and then wind, thunder and lightning. Our tiny boat rocked up and down waves and swells that rose much higher than the boat itself. They must have been twenty feet or more. I learned later that it was the outer edges of a hurricane sweeping though the gulf.

For some reason, no one else on the boat woke up. I was alone on the deck of this rolling vessel in the middle of a storm far out to sea. I could visualize the boat sinking under the crash of the next wave. I saw myself clinging to a scrap of lifesaver or deck railing. I asked myself, "Is this it? Is this how my life will end?" Finally, I just prayed, calling out God for help. Save me! I called out of my desperation and need to the one who was indeed coming out across the waters of the night to me.

On the tenth day we headed back to Carrabelle with, what we thought was a decent-sized catch, not great, but good enough for a healthy profit. When we got back to the dock however, we found out that the captain's second boat had separated from us and then secretly returned to the docks on the first day, on what seemed like a trumped-up pretext. But without the value of the catch of the second boat, our catch would never be enough to make a payment on the boats and pay all the expenses of both boats. Nothing would be left to pay the crew. All the captain's boats were repossessed the moment we reached the dock. All of our catch was taken as partial payment for the expenses, and the four of us on the crew received nothing.

The captain simply got up and hitchhiked out of town. He said he was going to Tampa where his luck might be better. The old sailor signed on with another boat. Angry and desperate, the other crewmember and I talked the fish man into giving us something for our labor. He handed us $25 each. My friend had to break it to his wife how he had been cheated. I got into my car and drown back to Tallahassee.

I think about those long days laboring to bring that long stringer of fish on board deck of the ship. I think the cool evenings eating fried fish and lima beans by the setting sun. There were the long nights alone sitting on the side of boat when all I could do was watch the rolling sea and the starry sky.

By the sea, I think I realized that God would always be a part of my life. Somewhere, deep in my soul, without words to shape meaning, without sounds to define its limits, I realized that my life had always been immersed in God. Like that small boat buoyed effortlessly yet uncontrollably miles and miles from shore, I was being lifted and dropped on each rising swell, held in grace between the deep and the infinite star-littered sky. My life was being held by God, carried forward on a wave, miraculously lifted above the churning deep which holds both life and death, below the majesty of God splayed out above, to see and give wonder, but not to touch.

I see now how those nights on the sea prepared me for the joys and the sorrows that lay ahead in my life. I see how God is thoroughly embedded in our lives. We are not like the ocean-born creatures to whom the sea so surrounded that they are never aware if its presence. We are not like the stars, burning away alone in space never touching the infinity beyond them. We sit in-between, privileged to see it all, yet propelled on, carried on the incalculable, unfathomable being of God.

The disciples were beset by the same fears. And then, they saw him, moving out across the waves, coming toward them. Who was this? Is it a ghost? A dream? An illusion? It was Jesus. And then he said to them, "Take heart. It is I. Do not be afraid."

"It is I" Three words in English, but in Greek, just one: First person singular of the verb "to be." "I am, me, I . . . " It reminds us of another single statement of being. Moses on Mt. Sinai before the burning bush asking, "Who are you, what is your name?" and God answers, "I am who I am."

Jesus comes to the disciples in the midst of a swirling storm of doom and chaos, and the forces of destruction rise all about, and simple says, "It's me. Here I am. I am here." Jesus comes to those who love him in their time of deepest need and deepest fears and assures them of his presence. He is with them in the midst of the storm.

You see, that's how it is. In the midst of all the storms of life, raging disease, injury and death, suffering, heartbreak, horror and fear, in the middle of all the rises to hurt and harm, to swallow us up in senseless chaos and destruction, God never abandons us, never leaves us on our own, never consigns us to the deep. God is with us, now and for always, God is with us.

But Peter was not so sure. It looked like Jesus, but how can it be? So he asks, "If you are really him, then command me to come out on the water with you." An odd request, and a familiar one as well. Remember the last time someone said to Jesus, "If you are Son of God, then turn these stones into bread . . . If you are the Son of God, then throw yourself down from the pinnacle of the Temple . . . If you are the Son of God . . . " Familiar words from the tempter's mouth. Not so strange then that a few verses later Jesus would tell this same Peter, "Get behind me Satan!"

Jesus responds to Peter's test by simply saying, "Come." Peter steps out of the boat, takes a step or two, but of course, the wind blows, the waves rise, and Peter begins sinking down. "Lord, save me" he cries. And Jesus reaches down and pulls him out of the waves. Together they get into the boat.

"Oh, you of little faith" Jesus says. We often take that to mean that if Peter just had had more faith, he would have been able to walk on the water with Jesus. If his faith had been stronger, Peter would have moved above the swirling chaos below. His faith would have saved him. But that is not what Jesus meant. Peter would never have been able to walk on water. Never. He always was going to fall. Only God can walk on water, and Peter was not God. No, Peter's lack of faith was his failing to trust that it was indeed Jesus who had come to them in the midst of the storm. Jesus said, "It is I" and Peter said "I don't think so, I'm not sure, prove it to me."

God comes to us in the midst of the storms of life, when death threatens, the hurt seems to overwhelm, and the loss seems forever. God is there with us. Take heart. It's me. Don't be afraid. The test of faith is not whether miracles happen, not whether we walk on water, not whether healing comes, or whether death is denied. That is not up to us. That is what God does.

Faith is knowing that we are not alone. Faith is knowing that we are not abandoned. Faith is trusting that God is with us. In the midst of the storms of life, we are lifted up and given new life, new hope, new joy by the one who was always there for us.

And when they all were back in the boat, the storm subsided, the winds calmed, and waters stilled. And they all fell on their knees and cried out, "Truly, you are the Son of God." Let it be for us as well.

4

ABANDONMENT

My God, my God, why have you forsaken me?
Why are you so far from helping me, from the words of my groaning?
O my God, I cry by day, but you do not answer;
and by night, but find no rest.

(PSALM 22: 1–2, NRSV)

THE VOICE OF THE ANCIENT Psalmist reaches out to us today, with
a cry that cuts to the root of how are truly are and what we have all
experienced. This lonely voice speaks somehow for all humanity
through all time. We all at some time in our lives have been deeply
compelled by sorrow, tragedy and pain to cry out to the God who
has promised us so such, who has held before us the dream of
truth, righteousness, justice, compassion and forgiveness. We have
all echoed the plaintive cry David so long ago: "My God, my God,
why have you forsaken me?"

This is the universal cry of every man and woman at some
time in their lives. There is something in the trajectory of our
lives that catapults us away from the secure and comfortable existence that we seek for ourselves. Something that forces us to face

loneliness, isolation and tragedy. Just as soon as we think peace has broken out, just as soon as we think loyalty and justice may prevail, we are rudely reminded by violence, by horrible circumstances, we are reminded of the frailty of life, the transience of happiness, and the illusion of security.

But the psalmist's anger and bitterness is not directly to the immediate cause of his misfortune. He is not betrayed by those who cause him to suffer. His psalm is a direct petition to God. "Where, in the midst of all that has gone wrong in life, are you, O my Lord?" He calls out to God even as God seems to be absent. He insists on God's help even as he seems helpless. He did not cry out "Woe is me for I am alone!" rather he cried "My God, My God why have you forsaken me?"

My grandmother was Leon Ouzts Brown. She was a very special person to me. She was my favorite grandparent. She was effervescent and alive. She was full of love for her family. She was the matriarch of the family in the very best sense. She was the "glue" that held the family together. Uncles, aunts, cousins, nephews, children and grandchildren, she held us all together. I grew up very close to her until I was five, spending many days and weeks in her care while my parents worked.

My parents moved to Florida when I was five and we were separated from our grandparents for long periods of time. Several times a year, we would make a pilgrimage back to North Carolina to visit all our relatives, but mostly it would be to visit with her. I remember so well with the first sound of car wheels crunching on the gravel of her driveway, she would come bolting out the back-door waving and smiling. She usually had an apron on, covered with flour from making biscuits. We would throw open the doors of our car, and come running to her, throw our arms around her and squeeze her neck as hard as we could. I could smell the sweet southern perfume that she always wore, get tangled in her hair net and cover her with kisses. I particularly remember kissing the small back of her neck where the short hairs grow, loving her with complete abandon.

Shortly after I had returned to Tallahassee after my fishing adventure in the Gulf of Mexico, I received a call that changed my life forever. It was a few days before Thanksgiving. The voice on the other end of the line told me that my grandmother had been involved in a terrible automobile accident. She was travelling to Florida with some family friends to visit us in Fort Lauderdale for Thanksgiving. She was sitting in the back seat of the car.

Somewhere on the interstate above Jupiter, Florida, a truck was being chased by the state troopers. That truck rose up over a small hill and smashed into the slower moving car our family friends were driving. They were pushed to the side of the road and stopped. Everyone got out of the car unhurt. But my grandmother realized that she had forgotten her purse on the back seat. She returned to retrieve it, and just as she did, the gas tank exploded into flames. She was trapped. The family friend reached into the burning car and pulled her out, but by then she was completely engulfed. We were told later that she was burnt over 90% of her body.

My father was the first to get to her at the hospital in Jupiter. He was the first to see her in the most extreme position of her suffering, the first to see the burnt flesh, the first to hear the screams of pain and the first to experience of the horror. I immediately left Tallahassee and drove to Charlotte where they had taken her. I don't know how she travelled that long distance in such awful condition.

When I got to Charlotte, I immediately went to the hospital where she was. My mother and father and other family members were in the waiting room outside the ICU. I went into her room right away. The heat of the room was overwhelming. A portable heater had been brought into the room to bring the temperature up to near body temp. A body with no skin cannot regular its internal heat. Without the heater, she would freeze to death.

She was lying on the bed covered with a sheet. Her whole head was wrapped in gauze with openings only for her eyes, nose and mouth. A suction tube had been placed in her nose down into her lungs, emptying bits of burned lung tissue into a glass bottle under the bed. One of her hands had slipped out from under the sheet. It was stiff and black. A young nurse who was experienced in the care of burn patients, was in and out of her room constantly.

My "Nana," as we all called her, was awake when I came into the room. Her eyes fluttered through the gauze coverings. Her voice was weak, but I immediately recognized the voice that had so many times in my life comforted me. I visited her in that room many times of the next two weeks. The first few days she was often awake and relatively free of pain. The fire had burned away all the nerve endings and there was nothing to feel. But as the days wore on, we were told that the nerves were beginning to grow back, and the pain was becoming unbearable. So, she received pain medication that kept her mercifully unconscious.

But the first few days of my visits she talked to me through the gauze that covered her face. She cried often. She pleaded for mercy. She asked why, why had this happened to her? She said that her mother had come to her, her mother who had died 37 years before. Her mother came to her and she begged for her mother to take her with her. "Take me with you, mama!" she said. But her mother only disappeared. "Why didn't she take me?" pleaded Nana.

On the second day of my visits to her bedside, the nurse came into the room. She asked if I would help her change the bandages that wrapped my grandmother's head and face. I agreed to help and together lifted her up to a seated position. Slowly we began unwrapping the gauze, round and round her head. There revealed to my horror was a head with no hair, no skin, just raw red meat, eyes without lashes, mouth without lips, a nose as only two holes in a skinless face. Nana looked at me through her agony, my heart broken in her eyes. As lifted her forward and removed the last of her wrappings around the back of her head, I saw one square inch of unburned skin on the back of her neck and the tiny feathered hairs that I had kissed so many times before.

Nana lived for a few more weeks. No one told us that that there was no hope of her living. No one told us that there was no way a person so extensively burned could live. So, as we held vigil around her bed every day that she was alive, we, her family tried to imagine how it was that she could survive. We tried to plan on going nursing care, healing and recovery. We tried to plan for a normal life after tragedy. We tried to resurrect hope from the grave of death. But there was no hope to be found. Nana died, without mercy, in her sleep after more than a month constant suffering.

"My God, my god, why have thou forsaken me?" Where are you in my time deepest need? Why have you abandoned me to the pit of suffering? All day long I cry out to you, save me! Take me away from this pain, take me away from this suffering, take me with you. And yet you leave me alone in the consuming fire. You leave to me to suffer alone. My God, my God, why have you forsaken me?

5

LOVE, LOVE, LOVE

IN 1975, I FELL IN LOVE, again for the second time, with the same woman. Marsha and I had grown up together. I have known her since we were ten-years old. We were in the same congregation, First Baptist Church of Plantation, Florida. We went to the same Sunday School, sang in the same youth choir, and were members of the same young group in high school. Our first date was the Homecoming dance our senior year, and we went steady for the rest of the year, ultimately going to Senior Prom together.

For college however, I went to Florida State and she went to Broward Junior College. Dating long distance was a challenge, weekly phone calls and letters, exchanging visits home and to colleges. But finally, we grew apart and broke up the summer after freshman year.

After graduation, I worked at home in Fort Lauderdale doing various jobs, door to door sales, digging ditches on construction, holding transit sight pole for a surveying crew, and sitting in the planning office of the Department of Transportation. The time period was the first few months after the tragic death of my grandmother after the auto accident. I was deeply shaken by her loss, traumatized by her suffering, and grieving at a depth with no words to describe. After a long period of numbness and surface level of feelings through college, my emotions were raw and laid bare. It was almost like the grief had pierced my shell over my emotions and for once I could feel again. The feeling were pain and sorrow, but finally I could feel something again.

My awakened feelings re-ignited my search for God and renewed my growing awareness of a spiritual calling. I heard, once again, the voice of God calling my name, calling me to come home, calling me to follow Jesus, calling me to serve God. So, I began exploring a seminary experience. I began to taste what it would be like to follow God for the rest of my life.

But my re-awakened feelings were not only the experience of sorrow and loss. I was open to feel everything now, the full range of feelings from joy, happiness, wonder, and curiosity, and especially, as I would soon find out, love and passion.

Later that Spring, I attended the wedding of a friend, Claudia Losey, who had also been a part of our high school youth group at church. And who should also be there but Marsha, as the maid of honor walking the aisle. We talked afterward and it was almost like we were meeting again for the first time. We began a conversation that would go on for the rest of our lives. As our hands touched that day, it was, as it is said proverbially now, magic. I fell in love for a second time with the same woman.

I went to seminary in Louisville that fall and Marsha came with me. We pretended to live apart, though in fact we were living together the whole time. Southern Baptist Seminary was a powerful transformative experience while it was also deeply learning experience. I learned about calling and service; I learned about loving, loving people and loving God, although almost none of that came from experiences at seminary itself. I learned about service at the hospital where I worked part time. I learned about the church while leading the youth in a church I served; and learned about love and life in relationship with Marsha at home.

After two years in Louisville, I transferred my degree program to Union Theological Seminary in New York. Union was deeply involved with the study of liberation theology, the confluence of theological study and the work for peace and justice in the context of the church. At Union I was able to cojoin my calling to witness to the suffering of humanity with God's vocation of justice and truth. Marsha and I were married the summer between Louisville and New York, and we came to the big city together in the fall of 1977 to begin a new life together.

River Region

"When the Son of Man comes in his glory, and all the angels with him, he will sit on his glorious throne. All the nations will be gathered before him, and he will separate the people one from another as a shepherd separates the sheep from the goats. He will put the sheep on his right and the goats on his left.

"Then the King will say to those on his right, 'Come, you who are blessed by my Father; take your inheritance, the kingdom prepared for you since the creation of the world. For I was hungry and you gave me something to eat, I was thirsty and you gave me something to drink, I was a stranger and you invited me in, I needed clothes and you clothed me, I was sick and you looked after me, I was in prison and you came to visit me.'

"Then the righteous will answer him, 'Lord, when did we see you hungry and feed you, or thirsty and give you something to drink? When did we see you a stranger and invite you in, or needing clothes and clothe you? When did we see you sick or in prison and go to visit you?'

"The King will reply, 'Truly I tell you, whatever you did for one of the least of these brothers and sisters of mine, you did for me.' (Matthew 25: 31–40, NRSV)

Loving God is not what you feel about God. It is what you do for God. Loving your neighbor is not how you feel about your neighbor. It's what you do for your neighbor. In the end, they are the same thing.

Her name was Christina. She was a Polish survivor of World War II. I came to know her while I was in seminary. In order to get through school, I worked in a large hospital for the mentally ill, one of the old kind, where they warehoused people who could not be taken care of anywhere else. The job itself had nothing to do with the seminary, nothing to do with a theological education, but I learned more about loving God there, than I did in any classroom.

Christina was a nurse there; I was an nurse's aid. I came in early in the mornings to awaken the patients, clean them up, dress and feed them breakfast. As I worked next to Christina, I got to know her life and her story. When she was sixteen, young and pretty, the Nazis invaded her town. They took her. She was not Jewish so she didn't go the death camp. But she was held in a building next to a camp, a brothel to be used by soldiers coming and going. Over the next years she was raped many times. She was never able to have children of her own.

After the war, she was held in a relocation camp in Germany for some months. She told the story of how one night, outside her tent, she heard the yelps of a dog in pain and fear. It was an unfortunate animal such as this that often became the next meal for the hungry in the camp. But this one got away. It ran to her for safety. She discovered its belly had already been cut open. She carefully stitched it together and over the next months, she nursed that pup back to health.

She learned some nursing skills there and at a nearby hospital, and she cared for a young American soldier who had been badly burned and wounded. That soldier later became her husband. After twenty-five years, their marriage fell apart. She was devasted, suffered (what was called then) a mental breakdown. She ultimately recovered, and living on her own, she worked at this hospital. But after all that she had been through, she was not bitter or destroyed. She was the most loving person I have every known.

The patients in River Region Hospital were ill with all kinds of conditions, schizophrenia, Alzheimer's, mental disability, psychosis, dementia, mental injuries. They were all grouped together on the same floor. They were usually drugged and herded about or locked down. They were treated as non-persons. But Christina never did. Each morning she would enter a room, call each by name. Though many could never answer or respond, she would ask how they were doing and sympathize with their needs.

One patient was an elderly woman. For some reason she was completely catatonic. Her muscles and bones were totally locked in a fetal position. The only thing she could move were her eyelids. Most of the staff tossed her about like a side of beef. But every day Christina would gently call her by name, lovingly tend to her bedsores. She would wash her body with a soft cloth and warm water. She combed her hair. She fed her with a feeding tube as though it was a grand feast. She dressed her in a gown and tucked her into bed, as though she was the most beloved person in the world. And for her, right then, she was.

Christina was not a saint. By her own description she was a lapsed Catholic. She never attended mass. She smoked too much. She had little use for the country folk she worked with. Through the isolation and abandonment that she had known in her life, her sense of God was sketchy. Small acknowledgements here and there. God, if God existed for her, was an idea without comfort.

Yet in her life I sensed more than a woman who had suffered much and still did good work. Perhaps it was just me. Maybe I saw and felt what I wanted to see. I was a young seminarian, who spend his time focused on theology and the Bible, struggling to find the call of God, and who reads too much of God into the everyday and ordinary.

Christina has stayed with me all these years. I still hear her voice and I still see her tender hands. And I still see her face. I could say she was like a Mother Teresa, without the robes, the prayers and the piety, hidden away in rural Kentucky. It was more a combination of all that she said and did, and all we experienced together. Her story wrapped up in mine. The faces from her past. The faces of women we took care of together.

In those years together, her life was a light to God for me. In her life, in her face, I caught a glimpse of the face of God, more real and more powerful than all the prayers or songs every sung. The gospel shown to me through her fragile and imperfect humanity betrayed the strength and endurance of love and compassion more perfect and divine than any words or sermons can convey. Hope was born again for me as she calmly wrung the warm water from her bathing sponge and so lovingly and so gently washed bodies of those discarded by the world.

I am convinced that the incarnation of God in Jesus Christ means nothing if it does not mean that here, incarnate in the lives of you and me, in the crazy mix of our dreams and weaknesses, in our brokenness and in the wholeness, we discover in the stories behind each of our faces, the shining human gospel of God. Here shines the human face of God seeking those who are lost, healing those who are broken, bringing transformation and resurrection to those who are dying.

Another patient in the River Region Hospital was Chester Netherton. He was housed on the men's ward for elderly patients. He was afflicted with Alzheimer's, like many of the other men on the ward, but he also suffered with emphysema. From the time I met him he was limited to his bed. He was cleaned and dressed, fed and clothed in bed. I spoke to him every day as I cleaned him, but in his confused state he never really made much sense, just rambling incoherent words and phrases. I was never sure if I ever connected with him personally. And every day, in every moment of the day, he struggled to breathe. The emphysema had progressively destroyed his lungs ability to process air or expel liquid. Every breath felt like drowning.

Over the course of the weeks and months that I cared for him his ability to breathe slowly diminished. His lungs were filling with fluid. On his last day of life, I and the other nurse aids working that day stood vigil by his bed. Every breath was long and labored. We watched as he drowned and finally, mercifully died. We watched him die right before us. We saw him stop breathing and the life drain from his eyes. His lifeless eyes stayed open, fixed on the ceiling. His mouth, no longer drawing air, hung open. His whole face was cold and pale.

The nursing supervisor soon entered the room, assessed the situation and then gave us our instructions for preparation of the body. We closed his eyes and mouth, removed his blankets and sheet, and undressed him. We took some warm water and wash-cloths, and washed his whole body. We were instructed on how to make a gauze square, coat it with Vaseline, and insert it into his anus to stop any leakage. We then took a clean sheet, wrapped his entire body, head to toe. We cinched it tight with another sheet. We left the mummy-like body there on the bed to be removed later in the day by other staff.

This was the first time I actually saw someone die, actually observed the moment of death. This was the first time I ever touched a dead body. My visceral reaction was one of complete horror--wordless, breathless, bone chilling horror. But it was at the same time an overwhelming sense of love. I was loving Chester as he died. I was loving him as I closed his eyes. I was loving him as I washed his body. I was loving him as I wrapped him in the death shroud.

In following Christina's caring example and in tending to Chester's death, I realized that this is loving your neighbor. This is loving God. They go together. You can't do one without the other. "Even as you have done it to the least of these," says the Lord "You have done it unto me." (Matthew 25)

6

NEW YORK, NEW YORK

WHEN MARSHA AND I MOVED to New York, we were quickly immersed in the vibrant, exciting life of the city. We took in the museums, Broadway shows, and concerts. We spend long days in Central Park. We traveled by bus and subway and took long walks on the West side, rode to the top of the Empire State Building and the World Trade Towers. We took the ferry to the Statue of Liberty, dined out in Little Italy, Brooklyn, mid-town and the East Side.

On New Year's Eve, we joined the crowds in Time's Square, watching the ball drop, marking the beginning of a new year. A few weeks later, we found out that Marsha was pregnant, and that very soon we would be welcoming a new life into our family.

Our first apartment in New York was student housing on the Union campus. But at the end of the first year, we moved to off campus housing. I became a building superintendent of a building very near the school on Clairmont Avenue. We lived in a basement apartment with windows looking out only on a dark alley between the buildings and with the bedroom wall being dark, raw foundation stones. It gave the feeling of really living in a cave. But the rent was free and there were no utilities or tax expenses, so living in a cave was financially a very good way to survive as a student family.

At that same time, we became committed to having a home birth with a midwife, a principled decision searching for an alternative to the dominant, patriarchal medical model of hospital childbirth in this country. As Marsha progressed in her pregnancy, we prepared for her to give birth in the warmth and safety of our home, attended by a skilled and attentive midwife and surrounded by supportive friends.

When the day of birth finally came, we all gathered in our home for labor. There was laughing and crying, walking and resting, breathing and definitely work as the labor progressed. And then after about 36 hours, Hannah was born. It was an amazing miraculous moment. The midwife received the new life and placed her on her mother's chest, and for a long, timeless pause, we were locked in infinite shared bliss.

And yet it wasn't very long before Marsha got up from the bed to take a brief shower to clean up a bit. I was laying on the bed next to her when she placed Hannah on my chest. There she was, laying stomach down, her head slightly turned. She opened her eyes and looked right at me. And again, an infinite moment of grace, a holy moment of such love as I have never felt before. My life would forever be changed.

Becoming a father changed everything in my life. It changed the way I felt about being a partner and loving husband to Marsha. It changed the way I related to my own parents and family and the way I engaged in my ministry and passionate relationship to God. It all became more personal, more intimate, more important, more essential, more compelling. My life and my ministry became a passionate expression of love for everyone in my life. My one reason for being was to love.

As soon as I arrived at Union Seminary, I immediately got involved with the movement for social change. Almost more important than my classroom experiences in my educational journey was my work organizing, educating and advocating for peace and social justice. I had already begun working against the death penalty while in Kentucky, so I continued that work in New York.

I became a member of the Fellowship of Reconciliation (FOR), based in Nyack NY, which was an organization that for pushed for non-violent action against war, violence and injustice.

We formed a FOR chapter on the Union campus and became active in direct actions on the streets of New York. I became a student intern at the United Nations working on the New International Economic Order (NIEO) project for a just and equitable system for the poor. We organized a rally for the first International Disarmament conference at the United Nations in 1978, which bought thousands of people to the UN to work for the elimination of nuclear weapons.

In January of 1979, I was ordained to the gospel ministry by First Baptist Church in Plantation, Florida. I had been examined and tested by an ordaining council of five other ministers in the local area. I was found "called" and prepared to enter the ministry. But as I articulated it then, it was not the usual pastoral ministry of preaching in a local congregation. I said that I felt called to the particular ministry of "peace and justice organizing," witnessing in God's name to the transformation of the world into the kingdom of God. As unlikely as it seemed at the time, those five other ministers affirmed my calling as authentic and commissioned me to be ordained a few weeks later.

And so, as a fully ordained minister of God in Jesus Christ, I began working for Clergy Laity Concerned (CALC), a national interfaith organization founded by Martin Luther King Jr. and other national religious leaders. I first worked at CALC as a program assistant, and later as the coordinator of the "Human Security: Peace and Justice for all," a program that worked for disarmament, human rights, and ending hunger worldwide. As the CALC staff person, I helped to form a new organization, the "Mobilization for Survival," (MOBE) a national coalition of almost all the peace and justice organizations in the US, coming together to work for the elimination of nuclear weapons and nuclear power. I assisted the religious coalition of the MOBE, drawing together national churches and religious organizations to fight a nuclear future.

I helped to coordinate for work of over 34 local chapters of CALC across the country. I visited chapters, spoke to the press, created campaigns and educational materials, pamphlets and posters. We organized rallies and demonstrations and practiced civil disobedience.

In 1980, a new strategy emerged in fighting for disarmament: A Nuclear Weapon Freeze. This idea, first proposed by Dr. Randall Forsberg of the Institute of Disarmament Studies, was a simple and easily achievable first step to a nonnuclear world. Simply freeze the levels of nuclear weapons held by all nuclear nations at the current levels, no more arms race, no first strike, no new missile systems, and then negotiate a gradual reduction of nuclear weapons from there. In other words, nuclear disarmament didn't have to be done immediately, all at once. It only needed to take a first step which was to freeze.

A great deal of excitement and support was generated by this new idea. People from across the political spectrum began to support this simple and easy way to exit the nuclear nightmare. A new organization was formed, called the Nuclear Weapon Freeze, or the Freeze Campaign. I served as the chair of the first executive committee of the Freeze Campaign. Long standing peace organizations endorsed the campaign and new support came from entertainers, musicians, local politicians, members of the House of Representatives, and eventually candidate for national office, Walter Mondale.

The new campaign was going to be the focus of the next big national rally for peace slated for the 2nd United Nations Disarmament Conference in New York City in 1982. As groundwork for the upcoming rally, CALC planned two educational speaking tours of peace advocated to tour various parts of the country. We planned and organized the "MX Missile Tour" bringing opponents of the proposed MX missile system in Nevada to speak about its dangers and problems. We worked with American Friends Service Committee to plan and organize the "US Europeace Tour" which brought peace activists from Europe to speak in the US against the placing of medium range nuclear missiles in Europe.

In the week of the Disarmament Conference in New York the summer of 1982, the religious committee of the Freeze organized a special, interfaith worship service and concert at the Cathedral of St. John the Divine. Musicians and faith leaders focused the worship service on the call for a nuclear weapon freeze. The day of the rally began with a march from the United Nations building at 46th street in Manhattan, through the mid-town streets with hundreds of thousands of people from hundreds of organizations, marching together, ending at the rally stage in Central Park. More than a million people were estimated to be present for this climatic rally of the campaign.

Following this major event in the Freeze campaign, organizing was catapulted to the local level, starting freeze campaign organizations in hundreds of communities across the nation. Support and momentum for the campaign grew daily until it became a major position plank of the Democratic National Presidential Nominating Convention of 1984.

In the midst of all this ministry of peace and justice organizing in the religious community, my life and ministry was total transformed again by the birth of our second daughter, Rachel. Like her sister before her, Rachel was born at home, an out of hospital birth. Although technically, she has not born "at home" because essentially, we were homeless at the time of her birth.

The building where I was the superintendent, our home, had been bought by Barnard College and was going to be transformed into student housing. In the spring of 1981, all the residents of the building were evicted to make way for renovations. We had to leave. I secured a building superintendent job at another building on the west side on Manhattan, but it did not start until July. So, we were invited to live with Carla Montagno, a good friend, until our new place opened up. Rachel was born there in an apartment on 78th street on the west side, which so happened to be the same apartment where the movie "Good Bye Girl" was filmed.

After many hours of labor, walking up and down 78th street, up and down the steps, back and forth in the apartment, Rachel was born, attended by a midwife, surrounded Carla and my sister, Ginger Burris. The cord cut by me, her father. And just as before, I looked into my child's eyes with wonder and amazement, overcome with so much love that I would never be the same again.

I loved her so deeply and so completely that my life would forever by overwhelmed with the love I have for my children. Everything I do, everything I say, every new direction I move to, every phase of my life and ministry, grows out of my love for my wife, my children, and now my grandchildren. It is all driven by, guided and directed by love.

John Gover

To live is to be engaged in the life of God. To live is to need God. To live is to be eternally recreated in the image of God. The only alternative is to die. The only alternative is to retreat back into the hole of isolation, to ask for nothing of life, to want nothing, to require nothing. The only alternative is to shrivel and die every day, alone need nothing and unneeded. The question then is one of degree. How much will we persist? How much will we struggle? How annoying will we make ourselves? How much courage will we be able to summon before God to insist on the things that are needed? With how much courage will we live every day, grabbing hold of its savor and engaging its dangers?

I had a good friend. His name was John Gover. In his life he brought courage, daring, vision and some foolishness. He had a hunger for every morsel that life had to offer. Good and bad, he wanted to taste life in all its richness and fullness. We went to the same church together when I was a teenager. He was four years younger than me. Although he would never admit it to me, I found out through his parents that he looked up to me, idolized me in a way.

Spiritually, I spent my high school years somehow trying to reconcile and keep together my commitment to the church and my passion for the popular culture emerging in the 60's. I tried to up one and involved in the cutting edge of music and styles and ideas. While I deeply valued the experience of God that I found in church, I hungered for "new" that was breaking out all around me.

Between my sophomore and junior year of college was the time I took off on a hitchhiking tour of the US and Canada. With nothing more than a backpack, a friend and I set off to find adventure, to find ourselves, to taste some of life by taking chances, to find something more than the security of college life. John, coming along a few years later, did much the same thing, only his passions were not so much religious but in literature and art. He had the same longing to travel, to push the edge of his life farther and farther.

John had more talent and vision than I ever had. I got to know him better after he was out of school. He came to live with us for a while when we lived in New York City. I discovered in him a writer of great talent. He had a buoyant, naïve innocence that took him into areas of life in New York that Marsha and I never dared touch: the punk scene, the artist's community, the writer's underground. We debated philosophy and culture, music and morality. Although I never promoted or encouraged the way he looked up to me when he was a kid, I always felt somehow responsible for John and the life he led later as an adult.

When John traveled, he always took what looked to him as the "road less traveled." He drove when he could fly; he biked when he could drive, and he hitchhiked when he should have taken the train. He made friends wherever he went. He traveled the world, returning with incredulous tales of the other side of the world most tourists never see. All of us knew that he was just gathering experiences for what would someday be the great novel of our time.

I share John's story here because perhaps I owe it to him, perhaps because there is an unresolved well of guilt in our relationship, or perhaps because I know I can't preach about the courage to engage life unreservedly, to knock on God's door without fear of rejection, without telling the story of someone who did.

While John was traveling in India, he made friends with an Indian man who traveled with him for a while, someone who served as his guide, his friend, someone who got him into some of those places most tourists never go. We don't really know what happened. Apparently, they shared a cheap hotel room in Bombay, and the obvious wealth of a traveling American was more temptation than this person could resist. They found John's body several days later. He had been suffocated in his bed. All his money and identification was gone. It was some days before his parents could be located and told.

John's parents were the most loving and gentle, the most giving people you could ever meet. I looked up to them and loved them when I was a teenager, and I grew to love them ever dearer as an adult. They never got over the shock and the horror of John's death. His loss devastated their lives. They never felt secure in their lives again. Their nights were haunted with fears for the safety of their other two children. I know their cry in the pit of the night was "O God, is this the good gift you have promised us? Have you snatched away our dear son and substituted a scorpion of grief?"

I had great difficulty bringing myself to face John's parents after his death. I loved them no less, but I didn't know how to comfort them in their loss, their loss that I felt so much a part of. I know I was not responsible for his loss. John's choices were his own. Maybe I feel guilty because my choices didn't end in tragedy, may because I survived.

There are no neat solutions to tragedies such as this, no easy appeal to scripture or God, that make it comprehensible and acceptable. We long ago rejected the notion that the good gifts of God only come in the sweet by-and-by. We expect the good gifts of God here in our lives today. We will have to wrestle with sorrow and loss, evil and victimization for as long as we live. Each of us are touched by it. Some of us will know its sting deeply and personally. We learn that the dangers of life are not to be toyed with: there is seriousness about this life to which we are called that removes adolescent sense of adventure and replaces it with a mature appreciation for the precariousness of each moment that we live.

We struggle with how to recover some sense of security. We wonder if we will ever be able to trust life again. Will we find betrayal at every turn? Will we be able to trust anyone again? Will we ever be able to walk through our lives with the kind of courage that lets us feel as if we had a right to be in it?

Grace and persistence fall together. Grace is ours in the miraculous discovery that we are children of God. As children we have the audacious right to stand for before God and ask for what we need. We fully expect that in selfless love and devotion, God our heavenly parent, will not trick us but will give us what we need and desire. Yet we must also deal with the reality that like the child tugging at the hem of the mother's dress, again and again as she does a dozen things at once, we must persist in asking God for what we need even when God seems not to hear or care and seems to have abandoned us completely.

As children of God, we by nature are a petitioning people. In our prayers and in our songs, in our life together as a worshipping community we claim our birthright before God. And so, on the other side of pain and into sober life of maturity, we re-emerge into life with a newfound security that drives us to keep asking the questions of life, that keeps is protesting the injustices and horror of life, and propels us ever stronger to trust in the lives of others.

It is a security, not that we will never be betrayed or never know pain or loss again. It is rather a security flying over the insecurities of our world grabbing hard onto the promise of God for the good things of the spirit. We don't know how or when it will be redeemed. We don't know when our mother God will turn from her chores and gather us up into her arms and shower us with the unconditional love a parent can give.

My friend John died much too soon. He trusted much too early. He relied on his daring and was caught from behind. But I must go living, and I pray that John's parents go on living, not frozen in grief and not balled up in fear, never risking or demanding of life again. I must grab hold of the promise that the bitter taste of the serpents and scorpions of life do not finally come from God. I must trust that through all the precariousness of living, God still has good gifts waiting for me. I must cling to my mother's hem, demanding, persisting, held high and safe, trusting this god whom I know as love, to see me through to the end.

7

THE VOICE OF TRAUMA

IN THE FALL OF 1982, I responded to a new direction in ministerial calling by accepting the position of Southern Regional Director of Amnesty International USA (AI). Amnesty International is a global human rights organization that campaigns for the release of political prisoners, the end of extrajudicial executions, and an end to the death penalty. My role was to create campaigns for those goals and organize local chapters of AI in the southern states of the US.

I did quite a bit of speaking at local human rights campaign events, held press conferences, organized local groups, raised funds for Amnesty International, and worked with other political and religious leaders to heighten the visibility of human rights issues. I met with President Jimmy Carter to join forces in a campaign for human rights in Africa. I met with Mayor Andrew Young of Atlanta in the context of the campaign to abolish the death penalty. I met with international human rights activist, Kim Dae Jung of South Korea, lifting up human rights concerns in Asia.

At this same time, a moratorium on the death penalty in the United Stated had recently been lifted. Executions were resuming at a frightening pace in many southern states of the US. In 1982 through 1984, I responded to over 13 executions in Georgia, Florida, Virginia, Alabama and Texas. We organized marches and demonstrations at the state capitals of many states, held multiple press conferences and press events surrounding the execution dates, and we held vigil and services at state prisons that held death rows and execution chambers.

I visited with several men who were awaiting execution, including Carzell Moore who was sentenced to death for the shooting of a convenience store worker. I stood vigil in 1983 outside the Jackson State Prison in Georgia at the execution of John Elton Smith. I also held a vigil in 1985 outside the execution of Roosevelt Green, Carzell Moore's co-defendant in the same killing. Green always maintained that he was innocent of the murder for which he was charged.

A few years later, I went to work for the Presbyterian Church (USA) as the marketing manager for the Presbyterian Publishing House. I really didn't consider it part of my ministry. It was just a job. I needed work and not to travel so much. We needed larger income that could support our growing family. Somehow the directors at the publishing house saw my experience in political organizing and social action as analogous to real marketing experience and gave me the job. I was happy to be employed.

I directed marketing campaigns for church school curriculum, denominational support materials like the Book of Order and the Book of Confessions, and miscellaneous presbyterian materials. I created catalogues, advertising, and direct mail promotions. I sold books and materials at the annual General Assembly. In truth, there was very little in this work that could be called ministry.

I worked at the denominational headquarters in Atlanta for five years. But while I was there, something very interesting began to happen. My relationship with the other co-workers in the building began to change, from co-workers going about the business of the church to something more like pastoral relationships. Some people would often come to my office just to talk, for counseling, for prayer. I began to relate to my co-workers like a pastor. Indeed, there was awakening in me a call to real pastoral ministry.

My ministerial calling was morphing from a call to peace and justice organizing to a call to preaching and pastoral care. This was made clear to me on the occasion of the death of a man who worked in my department, someone who I actually supervised in his work. In a whole building full of ordained presbyterian ministers, I was asked to conduct the memorial service for this man in there in the chapel of the denominational headquarters. I clearly had become a pastor while selling the goods and services of the church.

And so, when the Presbyterian Center in Atlanta closed and consolidated all the denominational staff and work into the new headquarters in Louisville KY, I left the employ of the publishing house and sought a call in a local congregation. I transferred my ordination from the Southern Baptist Church to the Presbyterian Church (USA) and joined the Presbytery of Greater Atlanta.

In 1989 I was called to serve as pastor of Clifton Presbyterian Church, a small but dynamically radical peace and justice-oriented congregation there in Atlanta. My past calling to organize through the religious community and my new calling to pastoral ministry merged into beginning of a new day of life in the church and a new understanding of how to serve God.

My Mother

My understanding of the nature and purpose of my call as a minister was singularly shaped by my relationship with my mother. I remember the sound of her voice calling my name; I can still feel the touch of her hands on my face and her arms wrapped round me in warm hugs; I can smell her perfume and powder on her neck. I can see the look in her eyes and feel her kiss on my cheek. Mostly, I still hold her love for me. My whole life, my character, my strengths and my weaknesses, my passions and my compassion, my vision, my ambitions, and ultimately my faith in God and my ministry, were all founded, shaped and sustained by my mother's love for me. She made me who I am.

My mother taught me from very early age that loving our fellow human beings was our first calling and obligation. I was always encouraged to love my friends and family, especially the most unpopular and marginalized friends. My very first friends in the neighborhood and at school were the ones who were rejected and pushed away by the others: a fellow named Jim who was a stranger in the next block; a guy named Billy who wore ragged clothes and didn't smell too good; and odd, skinny boy named Seth who was smart and athletic but who was poor and rejected; and a big guy named Bobby whose family was from France and whose foreign sounding name and awkwardness made him shunned by all the other kids. These guys were my friends. I simply loved them and made them my friends.

I was very close to my mother throughout all my childhood. We did things together all the time. I went grocery shopping with her, following her up and down the aisles. I cooked with her in the kitchen; she taught me her favorite recipes. I helped her clean house and work in the yard. She led me to church, sang hymns together with me. She taught me how to pray.

Even as a teenager when most kids are beginning to separate from their parents and establish their own boundaries and identities, I remained very close to my mother. That is, until an event happened when I was fourteen, that changed all that, an event that wounded our relationship and set a course for my independence from that day on.

Our church had a youth basketball team that played a regular schedule of games against teams from other churches in our county. One Saturday that year, my team was to play against the team at Pompano Baptist church, about twenty miles away. We all met at our church that morning to ride together up to Pompano. But for some reason, our coach and driver to the event didn't show up. What to do? Forfeit the game? One of the older kids had a driver's license and a car, so we all piled in with him and road to the game. We played and lost the game spectacularly without a coach and came home later that afternoon.

I told my parents what had happened. I was actually quite proud that we had pulled it off. But my mother was furious. To drive that distance in a car, packed with kids, driven by another kid, was beyond the pale. I tried to convince her that we were safe, that there was nothing wrong, that we actually had done well, but she would not hear of it.

The argument got out of hand. Finally in a heated attempt to inflict as much damage as I could muster, I shouted at her, "I hate you!" The world stopped turning. The air left the room. Then my mother erupted with a violent series of blows around my body, slaps around my head, driving me backward out of the kitchen, through the dining room, back to my bedroom. She wailed inconsolable tears and retreated back to her bedroom. I stayed a long moment in my room, ashamed of what I had said, ashamed of what I had done. I knew at that moment our relationship had changed forever. I had broken her heart. I rushed to her and held her. I cried and said I was sorry. But none of my pleading could ever take back those bitter words. And violent blows could never heal my broken heart as well.

Through the following years, it became clear that from that time on, I was on my own. The separation was complete. I was making my own decisions, walking my own path and there was nothing my parents could do about it. I made the decisions about school and studies, about clothes and hairstyles, about music, sports and entertainment, about church, theology and politics. I chose my college, my major field of study. Without their permission, I dropped out of college for a couple quarters to hitchhike all around the country. Eventually I came back to school of my own accord and finished a degree course. I ultimately made a life immersed in the being and call of God I chose my life's purpose.

After the death of my grandmother, my mother was never the same again. She carried a burden of grief and horror that would forever shape her outlook on life. The light had gone out of her eyes. She was always on the edge of tears. She continued to love me and my sisters with great power and passion. She welcomed her grandchildren with tenderness and grace. But there was always a shadow of sadness behind everything she said or did. In a very real sense, began dying on the day my grandmother died. My mother died of a broken heart.

Her actual death began 20 years later with the radical decline of her physical health. My mother smoked for many years and was never able to stop. She developed multiple physical conditions that eventually broke her body. She had serious early onset osteoporosis which led to weakness in her bones, a broken hip, difficulty walking and ultimately to using wheel chair. Her breathing was seriously compromised, suffering chronic bronchitis and led to a constant cough. Her circulatory system was weakened by smoking leading to capillary collapse.

She was hospitalized after she developed persistent rectal bleeding. For many days the doctors tried to find the source of her bleeding, but could never find it. One day I was visiting her in the hospital during this crisis. I was the only family member there at the time. My father and sisters had gone back to the house. Her attending physician brought me into his office and insisted that I watch the full video of my mother's colonoscope examination of her lower bowels. I experienced a kind of trauma at the visage of this too intimate view of my mother's interior.

I went back home shortly thereafter, and two weeks later my mother died there in the hospital. We all attended her funeral. Her home pastor performed the service. We buried her in a cemetery not far from their home in Plantation, Florida. I carry a great hole in my heart left by the death of my mother. The trauma she witnessed in the suffering and death of her mother, the trauma she herself experienced in the grief and horror borne for years afterward, and the actual physical trauma suffered by her own physical collapse and death, all combine to envelope the deep love I have always felt for her and cloud her memory with pain and sorrow. I weep for my mother. I weep for myself.

K. A. Brown

My mother's father was named Kurnell Aaron Brown. Like my other grandfather, he was also called by his initials, "K. A." He was, what is often called, a working man. He worked with his hands all his life. He worked in the textile mills. He worked in the fields. He worked maintenance at a local motel. He was a mechanic, working on cars and trucks all his life. For a while he owned a gas station in town.

Although Papa was a big man, he was always kind and gentle. I never heard him raise his voice in anger, never saw him raise his hands in violence. He simply lifted us into his lap in kindness and patted our heads in love. He entertained us with stories and jokes, and a simple song or two.

The back yard of his house was one big, working lot, with a work shop, garage, tractors and machines, old cars and a trailer. Whenever we would visit my grandparent's home, my greatest joy was to hang out and play in the junkyard behind the house. I often went to work with Papa Brown, riding shotgun in his truck, working beside him as he fixed things in the shop or at the motel. I learned the practical side of work from him. In many ways, I learned how to be in the world from my grandfather Brown. I am Papa.

Papa died many years later. He was living alone then, after the death of my grandmother. He did the same work in retirement as he did when he was employed, puttering around, fixing things, building things, repairing things. He went to church every Sunday, sang in the choir, served on the board of deacons. On that last Sunday morning, he got up early as usual, dressed for church, made out his check for the offering plate and put it in his shirt pocket. He sat down in his big overstuffed chair to wait for his ride to come by to take him to church. And there, peacefully and gently, his heart stopped. He died waiting to go to church. He died ready to go home.

Jenny Currie Burris

We all have had encounters with the holy. We all have experienced times when we have been drawn out of the ordinariness of living, plucked out of our routines and shaken, tested to limits of endurance, the limits of vision, the limits of strength. There are times when the shallow bottom of the everyday drops out to reveal an unexpected, and unfathomed depth.

There have been times when faces, people, and places drop their two-dimensional flatness and begin to shine with a depth and presence too real to touch, times when we have been gripped, wrestled to the ground, caught in a lock that wouldn't let go. That is when we are snatched out of the abstractions that play around our head, and we are forced us to deal with life in raw immediacy. There are times when an angel of God catches us unaware and claims our lives. Encounters with the holy.

On my way home from a worship conference in North Carolina in 1992, I decided to stop by Charlotte, the place where I was born and spent the first few years of my life. My daughters, Hannah and Rachel, were with me at the conference and I wanted them to see the place where I was raised. I also wanted them to see my last surviving grandparent, Jennie Currie Burris, my father's mother who was in a nursing home a few miles outside the city.

While in Charlotte we went by the house we lived in, the school I would have gone to, and we went to the grave of mother's parents who also lived in the area. As we left there and headed toward the nursing home, it somehow felt like we were going to visit yet another relic, another tombstone. I reminded the girls that their great grandmother wouldn't know them. She wouldn't know me. Alzheimer's had robbed her of her memory. At 92 years old, time had taken away most of her faculties.

As I pulled into the parking lot at the nursing home, the awkwardness and uneasiness of the visit set in. I hadn't seen her in two years and then she had slept the whole time. The last time she could really talk with any recognition was over ten years before. Who was I to visit now, to swoop in, out of convenience, to pass a few minutes and feel better about myself as if I had performed some real service? How dare I come, but how could I stay away?

We made our way to her room. I barely recognized her. I had to check to make sure it was her. Slumped down in her chair, I was stunned at how she had changed. She could make only repetitive mumbling sounds, but in her eyes I saw the grandmother I always knew.

I forced a one-way conversation with her, imagining what she might be trying to say. I talked about the times when I visited her house and how she always had a nutty buddy ice cream cone for me. I reminded her about how I played on her porch swing and how I ran for hours through huge house exploring. I remembered how she never cut her hair, and how at bedtime she would let down those long silver-gray locks that were so neatly tucked-up all day. I talked about the picture I had seen of her as a girl, and how beautiful she was then.

Through it all she kept mumbling and her eyes, those eyes that used to hold this small innocent boy, darted back and forth almost desperately, as if she were trying to communicate, trying to say something. It was then that the tragedy and cruelty of it hit me. I choked back my own anger, my own tears, and my own fear of being left like this. And then Hannah, Rachel and I held her hands and we prayed. I don't remember what I said. We held on for a while. And I hugged her and said I loved her. The girls did too, and we left.

I saw those darting eyes for a long time. I heard what was left of her voice. I felt the cool texture of her skin. Prayer never felt as real to me as it did just then. In that mixture of love and fear, in the coming together of age and tender childhood, both real and remembered, in a moment in my life where there were no abstractions, nothing to protect me from the tenderness and brutality of that moment holding her hand, I knew the presence of the holy. Not heavenly choruses, not angel choirs, not ecstatic visions, not with all the complications and struggles of life somehow resolved and dismissed, but in one tender moment crossing four generations, full of all that life really is, we were held in the arms of God.

My Father

I am James Currie Burris, Jr., named after my father, James Currie Burris. His family and friends always called him "Jimmy" I called him "daddy." I am called "Currie" to distinguish me from him, and while I fully embrace this name and love its uniqueness and link to Scottish heritage, there were times in my youth when I hated that name. It was often misspelled and mispronounced. Teachers were confused by it. Other kids teased me with it, twisting it in various insults and diminutives.

Once when transitioning from elementary school to junior high school, I tried to change it, and have everyone call me "Jim." But it didn't work; no one believed it. So, I stuck with "Currie" and I am now glad I did.

I always had a great relationship with my father. I loved him. I admired him and looked up to him. He taught me so many things about living, about growing up, about work, loyalty and dedication. I loved that he loved my mother. They often displayed open shows of affection, kissing, hugging, dancing together on living room floor for all of us to see.

My father was the oldest son of six children to C.C. and Jenny Burris. He was a veteran of World War II, fighting in the army in the Pacific. He was the only sibling in his family not to follow an academic or educational vocation. He tried to pursue a graduate degree after college but he dropped out of the master's program after a semester because he said he needed make and living and support his young wife and family. He became a salesman.

By the time I was in high school, it became apparent that my father had developed a drinking problem. His grandfather, James Taylor Burris, had been crusader for prohibition in North Carolina in the late 1800's, and his father, C.C. Burris, was a Baptist minister and a tee-totaler, never allowed a drop of drink in his household. But my father rebelled against this raising, and embraced the fashion of a modern household of 1940's America. He always had a cocktail before dinner. Then as the years when on, that cocktail became the martini lunch, scotch in the afternoon, and then again in the evening. I remember telling my mother one evening as I helped her with dinner that I would never drink, I would never be like my father. Curiously, she responded with how disappointed that would make my father.

Years later, after I had married and had two children of my own, visits back home with the whole family became increasingly difficult. My father would drink every day, and by early evening, and sometimes earlier in the day his behavior would become drunkenly boorish. I just didn't want to expose my children to this.

The worst however was his nightmares while sleeping. Every night while we slept in the rooms across the hall, he would cry out in his sleep, long mournful wails and whimpers. He would literally cry in his sleep. We all would hear it and could nothing about it. At the time we attributed it to his drinking, the odd effect of alcohol on his system, a kind of delirium tremens common with alcoholics.

But some years later I learned about the effects of trauma on human spirit and body. Today it is called "moral injury." Trauma need not only be pain and suffering that you experience yourself. Trauma can be inflicted by witnessing and sharing the experience of trauma inflicted on others. Just be being present as others are experiencing terrible things themselves, causes trauma in those who witness it. Watching someone beaten or punished, seeing someone racked with illness or disease, being present as some experiences the great pain and horrific consequences of war, natural disaster, famine, or accidental injury all can cause moral injury to the witnesses.

My father was the first one to arrive at the hospital after my grandmother's terrible automobile accident. He witnessed her terrible suffering after being consumed with flames. He saw things and heard things that no one in my family ever experienced. The trauma he witnessed became the trauma he experienced. He had a drinking problem before he witnessed her accident, but I am convinced that his full-blown alcoholism came afterward as a consequence of the post traumatic horror that lived in his eyes every day and every night from that day onward, until his death. The alcohol could not blunt the pain in his soul, and sleep could not silence the cries in the night.

The call came to me unexpected, my sister calling from a hospital in Florida. Come quickly. He is failing. He might not make it through the night. It didn't realize my father was so sick. Apparently, he kept the progression of his disease, cirrhosis of the liver, a secret from us, his children. He had fallen, been taken to the hospital, and now was delusional, hardly coherent at all. I got on the next plane, and arrived at the hospital in the evening. He was yellow looking. I couldn't understand anything he was saying. I think he recognized me, but I am not really sure.

But I held his hand, stroked his brow, and I prayed. I prayed for healing for my father, I prayed for peace for this dear soul from whom I came. I prayed for the one who raised me, who loved me, the one I look like, the one I love. I prayed to God to save my father. I prayed to God who was right there with me, holding my hand, holding my sister and my father and me as surely as the storm of coming death swirled around us in the raging storm.

Later that night, my father died, gasping for breath, blinded by sweat, delirious and confused.

In the midst of all the storms of life, raging disease, injury and death, suffering, heartbreak, horror and fear, in the middle of all the rises to hurt and harm, to swallow us up in senseless chaos and destruction, God never abandons us. Even though it seems like God is not there, that God will do nothing to intervene, that God is distant and unaware, the truth is that God never leaves us on our own, never consigns us to the deep. That is because in the darkest of times, God is there, suffering with us. Now and for always, God suffers with us.

8

WELCOMING THE STRANGER

Is not this the fast that I choose:
to loose the bonds of injustice,
to undo the thongs of the yoke,
to let the oppressed go free,
and to break every yoke?
Is it not to share your bread with the hungry,
and bring the homeless poor into your house;
when you see the naked, to cover them,
and not to hide yourself from your own kin?
Then your light shall break forth like the dawn,
and your healing shall spring up quickly;
your vindicator shall go before you,
the glory of the LORD shall be your rear guard.
Then you shall call, and the LORD will answer;
you shall cry for help, and he will say, Here I am.

(ISAIAH 58: 6-9, NRSV)

Night Hospitality

Just a little south of downtown, Interstate 20 makes its way through Atlanta. The Moreland Avenue North exit places travelers on the avenue headed back into Atlanta. About two miles ahead is an older section of the city which was the first suburbs of Atlanta almost 100 years ago. This residential area is a mix of small bungalow type homes, large Victorian style mansions, small apartment complexes, and newer homes built in the last few years. The neighborhood names are familiar to most Atlantans: Inman Park, Candler Park, Poncey Highlands, Lake Claire.

In the center of these neighborhoods was a small shopping area called Little Five Points, so named because five streets come into one intersection. There were small shops, banks, and a grocery store all gathered around a small, triangular park. But Little Five Points was more than businesses. It was a lifestyle, an attitude, an allure, a place to be. In the mid-sixties through the seventies, it was the heart of the counter-culture movement in Atlanta. Head shops, record stores, vegetarian restaurants, and whole foods cooperatives were a part of the scene. Young people were drawn to Little Five Points to be a part of something, to make a statement, to be different. If you wanted to be a hippie, or if you wanted to see one, this was the place to go.

Not far from Little Five Points, down McLendon Avenue in the Lake Claire neighborhood was Clifton Presbyterian Church founded in 1924. And for the next fifty years, Clifton was a small, friendly, intown church. Some people spent their whole lives attending Clifton church. People raised families there. Many had their funerals there. The membership was never very large, reaching an all-time high of 150 in the mid-fifties, but mostly averaging around 50 to 70 folk. In 1955, a large plot of land with a house on it at the corner of McLendon and Connecticut, came up for sale and the church bought it. They kept the house to serve as an educational unit and built a sanctuary adjoining it. In 1960, Clifton began worshipping there.

Ed Loring and Murphy Davis came to Clifton as pastors at a time when the whole country was trying to understand and recover from the extraordinary upheavals of the 1960's and early seventies. The civil rights and anti-war movements had a tremendous impact on the shape of American society. These movements also impacted the Church, religious leaders and their sense of the role of the Church in society. At first, it was only individual ministers and rabbis, and church members who were involved with these movements. But before the decade was over, major denominations were taking stands on civil rights and questioning the role of the United States in Southeast Asia. The rush of powerful historical events compelled people of faith to action and organized church responded.

By the mid-seventies, many people were beginning to reflect on what had occurred and to ask important theological questions. A whole generation of young seminarians and ministers had also been activists and protesters. Many had been arrested. The civil rights movement and the war in Vietnam had called people to action in God's name. But what was the connection between this new-found activism and the church and its traditional theology we had been raised with? What is the relationship between the Gospel of Jesus Christ and working for human rights, justice and peace? What does the Bible say about the relationship of the Church and the state, the principalities and powers of the political world and the emerging Kingdom of God?

William Stringfellow, in his book, *An Ethic for Christians and Other Aliens in a Strange Land*, developed the idea that the core of Christian identity is always to be outsiders to the dominant culture of the times. The voice of the Gospel is always to be a critique to the ways in which culture, politics and economics draws us into intentional or unintentional idolatry. If God is sovereign in our lives, then we must always reject the inevitable ways in which even the most benign forces of government, business, family and even religion itself, place themselves between us and God. This was a radical idea in a time where God and country were often seen as synonymous. But to many after Vietnam, Stringfellow's voice had the ring of truth.

Ron Sider's book, *Rich Christians in and Age of Hunger*, also had a powerful impact. Sider's analysis focused on the need to go beyond charity and handouts in facing world hunger. He demonstrated how North American Christians are directly implicated in the hunger of millions around the world through our dependance upon and manipulation by multinational corporations and their partnerships with powerful geopolitical interests. The rich lifestyles of many Christians in the United States depend, says Sider, on the poverty, cheap labor, and exploitation of millions of hungry people around the world. As Christians we are morally compelled to begin thinking about new ways of living and new ways of relating to our dominant culture.

At this same time, Jim Wallis and Wes Michaelson, two young seminarians, themselves veteran activists from the sixties, founded a new magazine called the *Post American*. From a radical, left-wing and evangelical perspective, they began calling the Church to move away from Christendom, the marriage of the Church and the state, to a new vision of a church freed from the dominant culture, living out the Gospel values of justice, freedom, simplicity and reconciliation.

The magazine was soon renamed *Sojourners*, and it became the center of an intentional living community in Washington DC and the voice of a movement across the country. They published articles by Stringfellow and Sider, the Berrigan brothers, feminists, human rights activists, ecology activists, simple living advocates, and radical theologians. They tried to link similar communities together. Sojourners was a place both for the spread of new ideas and for action. They helped sponsor rallies and demonstrations, and ongoing campaigns for human rights, world hunger, and nuclear disarmament.

Liberation Theology was beginning to be discovered in the United States at this time. Gustavo Gutierrez' *The Theology of Liberation* had been translated into English and was beginning to be taught at some seminaries. Sojourners began reprinting excerpts from such theologians and interviewing people like Dom Helder Camara from Brazil. Sojourners was the first exposure to liberationist thinking in a Christian context for many people in the Church.

Sojourners also helped revive interest in the Catholic Worker movement. The *Catholic Worker* was founded in the 1920's by Peter Maurin and his young protege, Dorothy Day. The Worker was a newspaper dedicated to the vision of Christianity in solidarity with poor and working people. Peter Maurin believed in the God-given dignity of every human being, no matter how poor. He preached against the forces of modern industrial society which quantified human worth based on productivity and which used and discarded people without regard.

In the Depression years of the thirties, the Catholic Worker opened houses of hospitality across the country, feeding the masses of homeless and starving wandering the country. They did this always with love and respect, and with the belief, growing out of the lessons of Matthew 25, that in serving the poorest of the poor, we serve Christ himself. The Catholic Worker movement redefined the understanding of the word "hospitality" from a kind of polite courtesy, to a radical embodiment of the Gospel in service to the poor.

By the time Ed and Murphy came to Clifton, Dorothy Day was in her seventies, but she courageously maintained her faithful life of service to the poor and her nonviolent witness for justice and peace. The Catholic Worker Movement was still a living model of the radical Gospel embodied in the modern world. Also coming to Clifton at this time were young people who had moved into the neighborhood, drawn to the countercultural image of Little Five Points. Many could be called hippies. They wore jeans and long hair. There were also veterans of the civil rights and peace movements. Some had been raised in the Church, but they couldn't connect the traditional religious experience of their youth with their new-found activism.

They found in Ed's preaching the connection for which they were looking. He criticized the U.S. government's complicity with injustice and oppression. He preached against the comfort of the Church and denominational hierarchies and their unwillingness to separate from the materialist culture of the United States. He called for a simpler, less formal church, and a more relaxed and spirited worship service. Once at Clifton, Ed reclaimed his own evangelical roots, boldly preaching Jesus Christ, but this time it was Jesus who was on the side of the poor, Jesus who lifted up the powerless, and empowered those whom the dominant society sought to crush. He called on Clifton to reach out to its neighbors and to find ways to serve the community as Christ would.

Before coming to Clifton, Murphy Davis had been active with the Southern Prison Ministry, and she found a receptive audience for that work at Clifton as well. Members began writing and visiting men on Georgia's death row not far from Atlanta. Murphy maintained an office of the Southern Prison Ministry at Clifton.

The first years of this new pastorate were exciting and renewing for Clifton Church and for Ed and Murphy. Membership grew and new life seemed to blossom. But this renewal was not without cost. Ed was a powerful and charismatic person. He had new ideas and he wanted to change many things. Air conditioning was removed from the sanctuary because it was seen as too luxurious and wasteful of energy. The pulpit was moved from the platform and placed as the same level of the people to de-emphasize the cult of the preacher. Chairs were placed in a circle for worship rather than in strict rows. Dress became informal with some people wearing tee-shirts and shorts and some going barefoot. With each change, there was often disagreement, particularly from the older members.

Many of the changes at Clifton at this time were an outgrowth of the Sunday evening Bible study. The focus of the study was not scholarly exegesis of particular passages. There were no lectures or outlines, no presupposed lessons to be learned from the text. Rather each study was open to the movement of the Holy Spirit, open to whatever God was seeking to teach the group that night. Most importantly, there was always an attempt to discover how the

Bible was relevant to our times. "What does this passage mean for us in our lives?"

As they delved deeper into the Bible, they discovered that the Bible had a powerful word for life today. They learned that their social concerns for peace, justice and liberation were themes woven all through the Bible. Traditional theology had tended to spiritualize these themes, but as they read the Bible again, this time with new eyes, a new and radical iconoclastic spirit emerged. The Clifton community discovered Isaiah 58 and 61 and its call to feed the hungry and to serve the poor. They discovered Luke 4 and Jesus' own self-proclaimed mission to bring liberty to the captives and to bring good news to the poor. They embraced Matthew 25 and its call to serve the least of these as we would serve Christ.

Each new reading and each new experiment in moving outside the traditional ways of being and doing church propelled Clifton to consider moving farther and going deeper. By 1979, Clifton was not the same church it had been in 1975. They were ready to do more. And the presence of homeless people in their community slowly arose as a challenge and as a call to mission.

One such homeless person was Joe Coppage. He had grown up in the neighborhood near the church, but at some point in his late teens or early twenties, he slipped into paranoid schizophrenia. As his mother found it increasingly impossible to deal with him, he began wandering the neighborhood. After she died, he became homeless. He would approach members of the church who lived near the church asking for food or cigarettes. He would sleep in their yards, or even on their porches, use their gardens as a toilet. He would wander into church services seeking food. He was obviously a bright man. Some have said that he attended Georgia Tech before his disease took over completely.

At the same time, homelessness was becoming a national issue. The economy was in recession, inflation was high, and many people were out of work. Drug use was on the rise, creating a wandering group of addicts in every city. Many states had emptied their mental institutions without setting up the promised community-based support, putting many mentally ill people out on the street with no homes, no support, and no one to care for them. The words from Isaiah 58:7 calling on us "to take the homeless poor into our homes," from Romans 12:13 admonishing us "to practice hospitality", and from Hebrews 13:2 which reminds us that "in welcoming strangers some have entertained angels unaware," all became very concrete. There were strangers, homeless people knocking on their door, and it seemed like God was calling them to action.

Clifton folks began studying the issue of homelessness in Bible study, through worship, preaching, and prayer. As a part of that discernment process, Ed and Murphy visited Maryhouse, a Catholic Worker house of hospitality for homeless people in New York City. They were moved and inspired by the witness of the Worker and the life of Dorothy Day. They began to think about the possibility of opening a shelter for homeless men at Clifton. In August of that year, Mitch Snyder from the Community of Creative Non-violence (CCNV) in Washington D.C. was invited to come to Clifton to preach. His message was powerful and direct. He said that there were people suffering and dying on the streets of Atlanta. "You have this room at Clifton, you have a bathroom, you have a kitchen, you have a washer and dryer. It would be immoral," he thundered, "if you did not open the doors this fall to the homeless poor of this city. There are thousands out there that need you, and this space belongs to them in justice."

On November 1, 1979, the night shelter opened and began welcoming homeless men each night to the church. The chairs in the sanctuary were stacked in the foyer. The pulpit and piano were pushed to the walls. Plastic sheeting was spread over the carpet and foam mats were placed on the floor with room for 30 men. The men's bathroom was outfitted with a shower. The kitchen was adapted for regular use. Ed and other members of the congregation took a van downtown and invited street people to come back to the church to spend the night. Initially it was hard to convince people to come. The first night there were only three men, the third night only one. But soon word spread that the food was good, the place was warm, and the people were really friendly. Before the end of the year, they were full every night.

Clifton was the first church-based, free shelter in Atlanta. There were no models, no well-worn paths to follow. They had to make up the rules and procedures as they went along, making mistakes and learning new ways of doing things. Soon volunteers from other churches were invited to come and help cook the meals each night and to spend the night with the guests. Food and supplies were donated or purchased from the newly established Atlanta Community Food Bank. An old school bus was acquired and volunteers began taking regular rotations driving downtown each evening, and taking the men back downtown each morning.

The first year was difficult and filled with challenges. Not everyone in the congregation agreed with this new mission effort. Some felt that the church was being taken over by the homeless mission. Some members left the church because of it. But there was also great excitement. The church was doing something new for God. There was a feeling that they were on the edge of a great movement of the Spirit, and despite the problems, God was with them. Other churches in Atlanta were also moved to do something for the homeless. Over the next two years, shelters were opened at Central Presbyterian Church, All Saints Episcopal, Oakhurst Baptist, and Trinity United Methodist in downtown Atlanta. It was the beginning of what has become dozens of organizations in Atlanta, including churches, non-profit organizations, and governmental groups, providing housing, food, advocacy, and supportive services for poor and homeless men, women and children.

By 1981, Ed and Murphy, and two other members of the congregation, Rob and Carolyn Johnson, felt the call to a deeper level of commitment to an intentional life of solidarity with poor and homeless people and with people in prison. They felt the call to break with a comfortable, middle, class lifestyle and its upwardly mobile professionalism, which segregated them from the poor and in many ways participated in the political and economic structures which made and kept people poor and powerless.

After a period of prayer and discernment, they decided to leave Clifton and establish an intentional living community which they called the "Open Door Community." Ultimately, they bought and moved into a large house on Ponce de Leon Avenue. They invited homeless folk and other volunteers to come and live with them in a worshiping community. They established a daily breakfast and lunch program, regular advocacy work on behalf of the homeless, and regular ministry to men and women on death row in Georgia.

Night Hospitality, as the shelter ministry came to be called, continued after Ed and Murphy left; indeed, it flourished. The core of volunteers grew to include regular teams from many churches around the Atlanta area, with over one hundred and fifty volunteers needed every month. Financial support grew through the years, coming from churches, individuals, the presbytery, foundations, and various government agencies which support services for homeless folk. Through such generosity, the budget of Night Hospitality became twice that of Clifton church itself. Paid staff were added to support and supplement the work of volunteers. The living space at the church has been added to and renovated several times.

No one ever kept count of the numbers of men who came to Clifton, but it had to be in the thousands. From 1979 to 2003, for over twenty-five years, there was welcome and shelter every night for thirty homeless men in the sanctuary of Clifton church, 365 days a year. But more important than the numbers, was the movement of the Spirit of God which makes Night Hospitality possible. A spirit of welcome and dignity greeted each man every night. A new spiritual community happened each night as volunteers and guests found God's grace together.

Night Hospitality started a process at Clifton that was unforeseen and unrecognized until many years later. Initially the hospitality ministry was seen as a faithful response to the call of God in a very specific emergency situation of homelessness in the city of Atlanta. It was understood that welcoming the homeless was one of those acts of compassion and justice that was a part of the life of radical discipleship to which all Christians were called. No one expected that it would continue to be needed many years into the future or that it would transform the whole nature and identity of the congregation so completely. And no one anticipated the new ministries which would flow from that initial call of God to welcome the stranger.

Soon another "stranger" was knocking on the door of Clifton. From the late 1970's through the mid 1980's the insurgency and counter-insurgency wars were raging in Central America. In 1979, the Sandinistas had taken power in Nicaragua but shortly thereafter, the Contras, funded by the United States, were fighting in the countryside. Wars of resistance and revolutionary struggle continued in El Salvador, Guatemala and Honduras. Government reaction in those counties was to fight not only the guerillas themselves, but also to target peasants, activists, religious and intellectuals thought to be in sympathy with the anti-government forces. The result was wave after wave of refugees fleeing all parts of Central America and seeking safety and asylum in the United States.

The Reagan administration sponsored a policy, through the Immigration and Naturalization Service (INS), which considered the majority of the refugees as "economic" refugees rather than "political." Refugees who came from countries with governments supported by the United States were rejected. Most attempts by these refugees to show that their lives were in danger if they were returned home were ignored. A flood of illegal immigrants, underground refugees, resulted. Many were caught and sent home where they faced imprisonment, torture and death.

Recognizing the inherent injustice of this situation, many church groups and individuals responded by offering "sanctuary" to these refugees. They illegally sheltered fleeing refugees in their homes and churches, hiding them from the authorities. Thousands of refugees found safety in church basements and pastor's homes. Many were transported north to Canada where legal asylum was granted. This was a new "underground railroad," reminiscent of the underground railroad which brought enslaved people north during the slavery days of the United States.

This new underground railroad also came through Atlanta, and Clifton Presbyterian Church responded. Along with the Friends Meeting House, Clifton declared itself a sanctuary church in 1985, the only churches to do so in the Atlanta area. Their intention was not only to provide a safe place for those in danger, but it was also to use the situation to educate people about the horrible things happening in Central America.

The first person given sanctuary at Clifton was a young man known as "Fernando," a pseudonym to protect his identity and the remainder of his family in El Salvador. He had fled after others in his family had been killed and after he had received death threats himself. Behind a bandana mask, Fernando and John Story, Clifton's pastor at that time, held press conferences and traveled to other churches and activist groups in the southeast to raise awareness of the atrocities in Central America. Fernando himself stayed in the homes of members of Clifton and of the Quaker House community.

Atlanta is not on the border with Mexico and consequently was not a heavily traveled stop in the underground railroad. Activity around the sanctuary and human rights issue subsided after a few years. But Clifton did play an important role in mobilizing the voice of the community for human rights in Central America. And the congregation learned once again that there is transforming and sustaining power in responding to the call of God, however that may come.

John Storey served as Clifton's pastor from 1981 through 1988. It was a healing and a growing time for the congregation. The church became known in Atlanta Presbytery as an activist and an evangelically-spirited congregation, eclectic in its worship style, outspoken on the floor of presbytery for liberal and left-wing causes, a thorn in the side of comfortable religiosity, and foolish in its willingness to flaunt denominational politics and convention to preach its understanding of the gospel.

By 1988 however, John was tired and he resigned to gather strength and seek clarity for God's call in his life. He later received a call to serve a church in Virginia, his home state. Patty Snyder was called as interim pastor for the year 1988–89. She was the church's first female pastor, but female leadership at Clifton was not new. Clifton had ordained its first female elder in the early 1970's, and women served in all major offices of the church. In the mid 70s Clifton had welcomed Christian feminist theology into its own practical theology and had recognized the empowerment of women as an important task of the gospel.

Clifton embraced inclusive language in its worship and preaching. They issued an inclusive language statement in 1986. While recognizing the difficulties of adapting the words of Scripture to modern understandings and recognizing the ways different people identify with and react to gender specific words in the Bible, the statement committed the community to struggle with and embrace new ways to refer to each other and to God.

I came to Clifton as pastor in May of 1989. It was a surprising and yet fortuitous confluence of ministries. I was raised as a Southern Baptist and was ordained by my home church in 1979. But my seminary degree was from Union Theological Seminary in New York City. After seminary I began a ministry of peace and justice organizing in the religious community. I was on staff with national peace organizations, organizing national campaigns and rallies. In 1982, our family moved to Atlanta when I became the regional director for Amnesty International. I helped witness against the death penalty across the southern United States for two years.

But as our family needed more stability, I took a job in the national office of the Presbyterian Church (USA) in Atlanta. I saw it as a job not a ministry. But while there, I discovered how much my own theology dovetailed with the Reformed tradition and how much I resonated with the Presbyterian Church. I also discovered a calling to be a pastor, rather than an organizer. Serving a congregation was where my heart was. And I believed I would flourish in the Presbyterian Church, something I could never imagine in the Baptist context.

Providentially, the timing of my search came together with Clifton's search for a pastor. One never knows exactly why a church calls a particular pastor, but I felt that I came to Clifton to do some specific things.

I came to help deepen the spiritual roots of the faith working itself out at Clifton. I wanted to help people claim their faith in God and Jesus Christ in ways that the liberal tradition often felt too embarrassed to claim. I wanted to raise up the power of prayer and to claim God's promise of healing--of the spirit, feelings, mind, and of the body. I hoped to do that through worship and preaching, through Wednesday Bible Study and prayer, and through pastoral care.

I also came to Clifton hoping to help the church attend to God's call to new ministry. Night Hospitality remained a strong and central part of the life of the congregation, but fewer members were volunteering, and new leadership was a critical need. Where was God leading now? What does that mean for Night Hospitality? How does Night Hospitality need to change to reflect what we have learned through the years and to reflect the changes in the congregation?

It was not long before another "stranger" knocked at the door of Clifton, a stranger who, it turns out, had been with us all along. Since the late 60's and 70's, the neighborhoods around Clifton Church had been home to a significant gay and lesbian community. Drawn by the alternative image of Little Five Points and the comparative acceptance of the diverse community already there, gay and lesbian folks found a safe place in Candler Park and Lake Claire. And there had been homosexual members of Clifton who were out and open about their sexuality since the early days of Ed Loring's pastorate. Clifton accepted gay people into the life of the congregation without a lot of concern or debate.

In the national Presbyterian Church however, it was a different story. In 1978 and 1979, the predecessor bodies of the PCUSA both adopted statements which named homosexuality as a sin and forbid the ordination of openly gay or lesbian Christians to the office of elder or Minister of Word and Sacrament. The vote in the two churches was very close however, and the debate raged on in the PCUSA for years.

Additionally, the Presbytery of Greater Atlanta was relatively conservative on this issue, creating a climate fear and suspicion. The homosexual folk at Clifton (most of whom were lesbians) for the most part were content not to rock the boat. Clifton was a good and healing place for them. They fought discrimination and acrimony on their jobs and in their families. Clifton was a place where they were accepted and did not need to fight.

Yet by 1989, the climate in the PCUSA had begun to intensify. Activists on the national level were pushing for change. Justice demanded that the church begin to include and accept fully those Christians who were called to the ordained ministry and were qualified by every other standard except by their sexual orientation. A national network of churches had formed to declare that they would ordain whoever God called to ministry without regard to sexual orientation. It was called the "More Light Network," the name taken from the famous quote from puritan pastor John Robinson, "God hath yet more light to spring forth from the Word." The network was small but vocal and growing. Another organization, Presbyterians for Lesbian and Gay Concerns (PLGC), was also pushing for constitutional change in the PCUSA.

Folks at Clifton began to ask if this was indeed time stand up and be counted in this struggle for justice. The issue was crystallized in the question of whether or not to join the More Light Network and publicly declare ourselves a More Light Church. Like several times before, Clifton began a process of discernment in 1991 which included home meetings, Bible Studies, retreats and congregation meetings. The debate discussed the timing of this move, but it also raised the issue of energy and commitment of resources.

The overwhelming majority of people at Clifton were in favor of ordination without qualification by sexual orientation. Clifton had in fact ordained homosexuals as elders in the past. We had sponsored a lesbian woman for entry into Columbia Seminary and supported her throughout. But Clifton remained a small church. There were only 34 members at that time. Energy for the existing ministries seemed to be stretched to the breaking point. Many talked of "burn out" and exhaustion.

At the end of the process, the session concluded that we needed to issue a statement affirming our support for open ordination and a pledge to work for change wherever we could, but they would not go so far as to join the More Light Network. There seemed to be no one willing to step forward and lead a new mission effort. There was no emerging group ready to attend meetings and put real effort into making our commitment more than a name on a list of churches.

That report was given to the church at a congregational meeting in the Spring of 1992. When the congregation heard the report, something changed. Most had assumed that we would join the network. While they agreed that we were small and did not seem to have the resources to commit to a large effort, the idea standing back with those either unwilling or unable to speak for justice was untenable.

Finally, one of our beloved elders, Melissa Tidwell, a lesbian ordained at Clifton, stood to speak. She confessed that for years she had felt safe at Clifton and had wanted it to stay that way. She did not want to draw attention to herself. But now she felt that time had passed. Now was the time for Clifton to declare to itself and to the rest of the church where we stood. She confessed that she herself needed to hear it from Clifton to finally assure her where we stood. She believed the rest of the PCUSA needed to hear it from us as well. It did not matter ultimately if we could not commit great resources to the struggle. For us, perhaps it was enough to be a name on a list. We should join the network and let the Spirit lead us from there.

Indeed, in her voice the Spirit had spoken. Clifton joined the More Light Network and became the only More Light Presbyterian Church in the southeast USA. A small action group did form afterward, and on and off through the years Clifton maintained a witness. Clifton was active in the local chapter of the PLGC, and attended three national gatherings of the More Light Church Network. Clifton folk spoke on the floor of presbytery and have written and sponsored overtures calling for changes in the constitution. Clifton served on a local presbytery sexuality task force and partnered with other like-minded churches in Atlanta as well as with predominantly gay churches. Clifton loved and supported gay members of the congregation. Clifton marched in the Gay Pride Parade in Atlanta, proudly displaying the Rainbow banner to the world.

But more than these external signs of change, joining the More Light Network changed Clifton as a congregation as well. It was a central part of Clifton's identity. When we talked about Clifton, most often we will mention Night Hospitality and More Light. The percentage of gay people at Clifton did not significantly change, but the congregation became much more intentional about being inclusive, more conscious of the language used around sexuality issues, more aware of latent or unconscious homophobia.

When Clifton became a More Light church, only two people left the congregation over the issue, indicating a broad agreement, but not unanimity. But then worship prominently featured banners with pink triangles, the More Light affiliation was printed on every bulletin, every new staff person was made aware of the church's position and while not requiring agreement, there must be some degree of comfort around the issue in order to be hired. In other words, for Clifton, the issue was settled; our identity was shaped by being More Light from then on.

Significantly, the youth of the church strongly identified with the issue. Although none of them had come out as gay when we joined the network, they nonetheless were proud of being More Light. Several had gay friends and they rallied around our position as a justice issue. In the mid 1990's when congregational interest was losing steam, the youth group led the church in building awareness of homophobia and in building sensitivity. They produced a play entitled "Coming Out, Coming Home," a radio play of coming out stories from gay, lesbian and bi-sexual youth. They performed it at Clifton and other places in Atlanta. One of the youth came out as bi-sexual. She made her coming out statement to us and to the world on the floor of presbytery during the debate over the ordination of gay and lesbians to the office of elder and minister. A very courageous thing to do.

Clifton had not become what some people refer to as a "gay" church. The percentage of homosexual folk who were part of Clifton remained at about 10–15%. With a total membership of 45, that is not very many. Gay and lesbian people came to Clifton for different reasons: some because they have grown up Presbyterian and want to worship in an inclusive Presbyterian Church; some saw the ad in the local gay paper and liked what they have found; some had been invited by a friend. Some joined Clifton because they specifically did not want to be in an all-gay church. They did not want to be segregated either by choice or not. Some resonated with the unique worship style and strong mission commitment of Clifton.

In 1995, the General Assembly passed changes in our constitution which explicitly forbade the ordination of open and practicing homosexuals. Churches which violated this ban were open to disciplinary action, even to the point of removing the pastor or replacing the session. The congregation showed no signs that it was interested or willing to back away from its previous commitments to inclusion, even though in so doing it risks such disciplinary action. No one actually ever took steps against Clifton. The consensus of the church was to go forward, following the Spirit as they perceived it moving among us, trusting in God with faith in Jesus Christ.

In later years some new "strangers" knocked on Clifton's doors. Several folk with physical and emotional disabilities became part of the congregation. One young man spent 19 years in an institution for the mentally disabled. He was misdiagnosed when he was one-year-old. They released him near his twentieth birthday after they had discovered their mistake, but only after he had sustained a number of physical and emotional problems that had developed over the years of his institutionalization. He had become self-abusive, injuring himself many times, destroying his nose, damaging his eyes, fingers, arms and legs.

Since coming to Clifton, he had moved out on his own, finished high school, and looked for work. Clifton accepted, loved and supported him through surgeries, struggles with the supportive services bureaucracy, personal struggles of faith. He was baptized at Clifton. He helped on committees, and he even preached on one Sunday, telling his story of struggle and faith.

Clifton welcomed others with physical disabilities, as well. People with severe injuries, on crutches or using wheelchairs, people with amputations, people with cerebral palsy and with polio, all came to Clifton in its final years. The church added wheelchair ramps and accessible toilets and showers. It changed the language in worship, understanding how words sometimes enforce prejudices about disabilities.

But the most challenging "stranger" to knock on Clifton's doors was the final stranger: death. Over several years, the church walked with two women as they lived with breast cancer. One was a long-time member of the church and the other someone who became a part of the community only after she was diagnosed. With each one, Clifton people hoped and prayed. They were with them through surgeries, through chemo-therapy, through times of great expectations, and times of great sadness and loss. Clifton had special healing services, special times of prayer vigils; the congregation sang songs of hope and songs of mourning.

In spite of all efforts, death still came through the door. Yet through it all, there was a miraculous sense of healing and grace. Both of these brave women, each in their own way, gave the community a great gift. They fought for their lives, but they accepted as a part of it, their death.

In addition to these losses, two young couples in the congregation lost children not long after their births. One family had twins, born very prematurely, who bravely clung to life, but who died after sustaining internal injuries not compatible with life. The other family lost their child at seven months. She was born with a form of spinal muscular atrophy that gradually paralyzed all her muscles, until she succumbed and died. Both the children and the parents in each of these situations showed incredible courage and faith. They were teachers of grace even as they bore their own suffering, learning to praise God and give thanks.

And the ones who were left behind learned once again that suffering is a part of life, that it does not have to defeat you, that God is with us even in the midst of pain and suffering, and that the love of God and its bountiful mercies surround us even in the presence of death. Clifton learned how to welcome death, the most fearful stranger, into our lives as a congregation and into the life of God.

The people of Clifton Church began to see that there was a connection between Night Hospitality, Sanctuary, More Light, and the ministry with people with disabilities. These major moments in the life of church were more than the expressions of liberal theological ideology, more than cultural, religious fashion or attempts at political correctness. Each of these was a response to the call of God to welcome the stranger. At each point, someone different knocked on the door of Clifton Church, someone who was outside our usual, comfortable network of relationships. They came seeking safety, refuge, a place of dignity and respect, a place to be accepted, and a place to worship God. And at each point, Clifton's response was not always immediate or sure, but eventually the call to hospitality was embraced as the call of the gospel, and Clifton rediscovered itself and was transformed in the process.

Clifton learned something about welcoming. They learned that it was essential to the movement of God. Breaking down walls and barriers is a primary action of the in-breaking Kingdom of God. For Clifton to stay the church, it must always be a wall-breaking, barrier-dissolving, ever-renewing fellowship. To welcome is to change, and to change is to make ready for God.

Lucy Rose

O LORD, you are my God;
    I will exalt you; I will praise your name;
    for you have done wonderful things,
    plans formed of old, faithful and sure. (Psalm 25: 1 NRSV)

While serving at Clifton Church, I had the honor of being the friend and pastor of Lucy Rose. She was a Presbyterian pastor herself, and a professor of preaching at Columbia Presbyterian Seminary in Decatur. She was a member of our church and attended worship on most Sundays. Having a professor of preaching listen to your sermons every Sunday could have been quite intimidating. But Lucy never judged when she was at church. She came to worship and serve God and was always very gracious in life and witness.

In Clifton Lucy found the kind of worshipping community she was looking for. She like the informality, the flexibility and openness to experiment in worship. She liked the non-hierarchical structure of worship where the chairs were placed in the round and many voices are welcomed as part of the worship experience. The concept of the "roundtable pulpit" would ultimately form the core of her doctoral dissertation and her first book, Sharing the Word: Preaching in the Roundtable Church.

But she was most impressed by the Night Hospitality mission and its relationship to the congregation. There was a beauty and simplicity about it that she always found very powerful and spiritually compelling. She often said the presence of the guest's mats, stacked at the rear of the sanctuary during worship was one of the most powerful images she had ever experienced. As long as the mats were there, worship could never become too far separated from the poor and marginalized people of the world. Clifton could not drift away into its own self-absorbed experience. While the mats were there, Clifton would remain open and vulnerable to the pain, and open to the formation of the new community that God is always calling together.

Lucy met and married Gerry Cook at Clifton Church. He shared with her this same vision of a worshipping and serving community. Together they got very involved in the life of the church, leading worship occasionally preaching, and volunteering with the Night Hospitality ministry. Deeply believing in community, they wanted to expand their family. At first, they tried to have a child. But that failed after several attempts, and they were drawn to the words from Isaiah 58: 6–7 "Is this not the fasting that I choose . . . to bring the homeless poor into your house." To Lucy and Gerry this was a simple directive and answer to their prayers. Their house was larger enough to accommodate two more people, they thought, so they invited two men from the shelter to come live with them. It was two men they had come to know and love through their work there. It seemed like the obedient thing to do and the right thing for them.

Louie and Dean came to live in their home as new members of the family. They were not a social project or an attempt at redemption. Lucy and Gerry set up basic ground rules for living together, sharing of chores and responsibilities, no smoking in the house, and no drinking at home. Both men had been long-term alcoholics. Louie had just returned from extended treatment at a TB center. After he came to live with Lucy and Gerry, he never drank again. Dean, however, had been as active drinker since he was twelve years old. It was the only identity he had ever known. He had long ago stopped believing in himself or his ability to be anything other than a "drunk" as he often described himself. But Lucy and Gerry didn't try to change him. They only agreed to love and accept him as a part of their family no matter what.

It took a long time for Dean to trust that love. He tested it many times, and each time they have accepted him back home. Lucy and Gerry did not follow the rules of the twelve step recovery methods. Intuitively they know it did not work for some people like Dean, who had been in and out of many programs. They simply resolved to follow the Spirit's leading and do all that they humanly could to make it work. Amazingly, Louie and Dean were a part of the household for many years, until both of them died years later in the mid 2000's.

Shortly after Louie and Dean came to live with Lucy and Gerry, Lucy became pregnant. In 1989, Lucy and Gerry welcomed a new member of their family, Lucy McIlwaine Cook, or "Lucy Mac" as she was called. Lucy Mac grew up in a house where, in addition to her loving parents, she had two other adults living with her who are as attentive and caring as any uncles or grandparents.

She grew up living and understanding community on a level that most people can only talk about. To her, Louie and Dean were not homeless men who have been taken in, but they were accepted parts of the only family she ever knew.

The community of Clifton church shared this journey of faith with Lucy and Gerry. The church community was the context out of which their decisions were made. The church supported and love them through the ups and downs of this commitment. Their life as a family was very much at the center of Clifton's life. Louie and Dean worshiped at Clifton, and Dean became an official member. When he was asked by the session if he believed and trusted in Jesus as his Savior, he answered, "As much as I can." This refreshingly honest answer matched the experience of others and he was welcomed as a new member. Dean and Louie were employed by the church at times. Lucy Mac grew up in a church where all this was normal.

Through the years, Lucy was a strong and guiding presence in the congregation. For many years she could not be active as a volunteer because of work on her dissertation, but she was always there at worship. She shared her life in prayer time, and she shared her heart and her prayers with everyone who sought her out. One of the "Lucy" stories that is always told, is that if Lucy said she would pray for you, you knew that she was not just saying that. Everyone knew that you were added to her prayer list and on that very day she would bring your name before God. Lucy was deeply loved as anyone ever at Clifton.

In June of 1993, Lucy was diagnosed with breast cancer and had a mastectomy. She underwent extensive chemotherapy and radiation. She lost her hair. As a show of support and good humor, the seminary celebrated a "Hat Day" where everyone on campus wore a hat like she did. Clifton did the same the following Sunday. All the family and communities in her life, including Clifton the Community of Hospitality, and the seminary, walked with her through that difficult time. By the end of the year, the doctors declared her in remission.

But in the Spring of 1996, Lucy began experiencing a persistent backache. Eventually she was told that the cancer was back and it had spread. Over the course of the following year, she had the standard rounds of chemo and radiation. She took experimental drugs, some of which had terrible side effects. She educated herself on holistic approaches and drank purified water. Eventually her family pooled their resources and sent her for a three-week stay at an unconventional clinic in Mexico.

From the very beginning of this odyssey, however, Lucy did what she always did. She prayed. She consciously and courageously gave her life into God's hands. She told everyone around her that she was willing to accept whatever God had for her in the course of this disease. If she was to live, she would praise God. If she were to die, she would likewise praise God.

In 1993, she preached a sermon at Clifton reflecting in her struggle with cancer. The sermon was based on the story of the man born blind in John 9. She concluded along with Jesus, that the issue with the blind man was not who was to blame for his blindness. The issue with her cancer was not how it happened, or who was to blame. The issue was not genetics, behavior, environment or diet. The issue for all of us as we confront life and death is to find a way to praise God. As creatures, we are born to be in relationship with our Creator, to lift our hearts in praise of God. Lucy found the courage and the freedom to face cancer through prayer and praise of God. In so doing she gave a tremendous blessing to all of us who loved her and sought to walk with her through her suffering.

Through the summer of 1996, into the fall of 1997, Lucy's life was marked by increasing levels of pain. Initially the pain medications were able to control it. Doses were raised. Combinations were tried. But as the pain increased Lucy's body gradually became weaker. The special diet she tried at the end of 1996 seemed to weaken her still. But through it all, she maintained her teaching schedule at Columbia. Eventually she was not able to attend worship as often as she like, but she always sent her love and thanks for everyone's prayers and support.

By the spring she was increasingly homebound monitoring her strength and energy so that she could still teach and do the things most important to her. More and more, people began to bring meals by her home and to stop by and visit and pray with her. Support networks were organized for Gerry and Lucy Mac. With the help of the faculty and students, Lucy was able to finish teaching her spring semester classes. By June, Lucy spent most of her days in bed. The levels of pain were raising requiring regular does of strong narcotics. A good friend of Lucy's, Marilyn Washburn, who is a minister and a medical doctor, began coming by the home almost daily to monitor her condition and administer her medications. To most around her, it was clear she would not survive the summer.

Yet Lucy's spirit was strong. A year before, she had started a daily journal which chronicled the events of her life and the inner struggles and observations of her soul. In it, she shares her ups and downs, she talks about scripture, she talks about things to do, and she prays. Regularly she surrenders her life into God's hands, trusting God's grace and loving presence through it all. This journal was later published as Songs in the Night: A Witness to God's Love in Life and in Death.

In a final letter she wrote to her friends and family, she said:

> "As I learn to live not day to day but hour to hour with pain and weariness, I am growing more and more aware of the such affirmations as "I believe in the holy catholic church, the communion of saints, the forgiveness of sins, the resurrection of the body, and life everlasting." Each affirmation points to a reality or network of realities that ground my faith. God is becoming the one I know as Jesus of scripture, whose life and love have been poured into my heart through the Holy Spirit. I am experiencing the deep immanence of God within me, the incarnation in me of God's life that it is no longer I who live, but Christ who lives in me. Especially I am aware that life within me that arises as the gift of the Holy Spirit is everlasting and cannot be snuffed out.

"This life draws me deep into God's love and into the bonds that constitute our lives together as a community of believers. To die is to gain—to be fully alive in God's unfathomably loving presence. But I believe I am not right now being called to die but to live this earthly life as abundantly as I am able—loving those I have been given to love, teaching and learning from co-learners in the classroom, and glorifying God, sometimes with my doing but more often with my being." (*Speak Lord, I'm Listening*, p. 309)

The last days of Lucy's life were a luminous, holy time, a time set apart from the ordinary in which all who were a part of her life experienced a very special gift, a special grace. Marilyn Washburn, her doctor told everyone that the time was near. Almost spontaneously people began to gather each evening on Lucy and Gerry porch after dinner. There were songs and prayers, short visits with Lucy who could not leave her bed. But the door to her room was kept open so the sound of singing of her favorite songs and hymns could make its way back to her. Friends came in from all over the country. Each had some time with her, and some time to gather with her community to cry, to pray and to sing. The sing was not dirge-like. It was strong and Spirit-filled. We sang some like "What A Friend We Have in Jesus" and "Be not Afraid" and "I'll Fly Away." Lucy always sent her thanks.

One time she drew Marilyn to her and said, "The important thing for me is that God is so magnificent . . . come to walk among us . . . knows the depth of our suffering . . . and loves us and loves us and loves us."

On the last night, the singing went deep into the evening. After most had to go home, a small group of friends gathered around her bed and sang whatever she requested. Lucy sang or mouthed the words as she was able. She lapsed in and out of consciousness through the night, and died at 6:02 am. Her family and close friends gathered round and sang the doxology, "Praise God from whom all blessings flow . . . "

Word spread rapidly the next day. Because a doctor was present at her death, her body could remain at home for a time. All through the day people came by the house and were able to go to her room and spend some time with her to say goodbye. And again, people gathered on the porch to cry, to grieve, and to sing. At the end of the day when it was clear that everyone who wanted to had come by, the funeral home was called. Her body was placed on a gurney, a blanket over her except her face. As she was wheeled out, over fifty people lined the sidewalk leading out of her home. Gerry and Lucy Mac followed behind, silently screaming in pain. The song was "I'll Fly Away." We sang, we cried, we prayed.

Joe Coppage

"When the Son of Man comes in his glory, and all the angels with him, then he will sit on the throne of his glory. [32] All the nations will be gathered before him, and he will separate people one from another as a shepherd separates the sheep from the goats, [33] and he will put the sheep at his right hand and the goats at the left. [34]

Then the king will say to those at his right hand, 'Come, you that are blessed by my Father, inherit the kingdom prepared for you from the foundation of the world; [35] for I was hungry and you gave me food, I was thirsty and you gave me something to drink, I was a stranger and you welcomed me, [36] I was naked and you gave me clothing, I was sick and you took care of me, I was in prison and you visited me.' (Matthew 25: 31–37, NRSV)

This story really happened. It is a Christmas story, a story of magic, a story of wonder, a story of redemption. It's the story of Christ coming into our lives right now, right when we need it most.

Night Hospitality was the shelter ministry for homeless men in Atlanta. It was based at Clifton Presbyterian Church. Every evening, 365 days a year, a bus brought 30 homeless men back to the church where they received a meal, a warm shower and a place to sleep on a mat the floor of the sanctuary of Clifton Church.

One year shortly after Thanksgiving, during the weekly meeting, the guests of the shelter decided that, in gratitude for the help and assistance they had received, they wanted to give something back. But none of the men had any money or any possessions, no more than the clothes on their backs. Nonetheless they wanted to give something. They had heard of needy families receiving assistance at Christmas. So, these homeless men decided to adopt a family of their own and try to make their Christmas something special.

Every evening as the men came back to the church, they dropped the coins they had collected during the day into a can on a chair by the door. At first it wasn't very much, but every evening the total grew. A few dollar bills found their way into the can. As word got around about what the men were doing, money started to come in from other folks around the church community.

A young family was found, a mother and three children, who would not have had a Christmas at all that year. As the days grew closer to Christmas, the amount of money in the bucket, collected from these homeless men exceeded $500. They divided into teams and went shopping, one team for the mom, another for each of the children.

On Christmas morning, the men put their mats and bedrolls in the corner of the sanctuary. Packages were wrapped and placed under the decorated tree. The young family arrived at the church later that morning. While everyone sang "Joy to the World," packages were opened. The kids rode their new bikes in the church parking lot. With weeping and laughing, singing and praying, those who had nothing gave to those who had nothing.

One of the homeless men gathered around the tree that morning hung back from the singing and celebration. He had come into Atlanta from a small town in Alabama. He had come to the big city in need of work and medical treatment, which was not available for him at home. He had left his wife and small children there. But Atlanta didn't work too well for him. He found no work there; no doors open for the treatments he needed, and months later he found himself walking the streets homeless, penniless and sick. As he saw the young mother and her children gathered around the tree, all he could think of was his family he thought he would never see again.

Later that night after everyone else was asleep, he got up from his mat and went into the bathroom alone. He broke open one of the plastic razors provided for shaving, and was determined to slit his wrists and end his life, there in the cold bathroom light on Christmas.

But there was another man in the shelter. His name was Joe Coppage. Joe was the first resident of the shelter when it opened 15 years before. He was a schizophrenic who had wandered the church neighborhood and slept on church members' front porches. Joe inspired the church to open its doors as a place of hospitality and welcome to the poorest of the poor.

Every night since then, as other homeless men came and went, Joe kept returning. In his mental illness, it wasn't always easy to understand what Joe was saying, what he needed or wanted. He never cooperated with attempts to find him a permanent home or treatment for his illness. But at the end of almost every attempt at conversation, Joe would end with a request. "Pray for me, will ya? Just pray for me?" And he wouldn't leave until you assured him that he was in your prayers. I always asked him to pray for me too.

That Christmas night, just as the man from Alabama had reached the end of his rope, as he was ready to end his life in despair, Joe came bouncing into the bathroom. He didn't know this man, maybe had never spoken to him. He did not know anything about his circumstances, his need, or even what he was about to do. But Joe just looked at him and said, "Ya know, ya know, Jesus was homeless too, ya know. Jesus was homeless, too." With that Joe turned around and left. Alabama put down the blade, turned out the light and went back to bed.

The next day he told me what had happened. He told me of how on a cold winter's night, in the chill of bathroom light, God came bursting into his life through a bathroom door in the form of homeless man. He told me how he regained his hope, how God's presence became real for him that night. He told me he would live.

Over the next few weeks his health got better, he got stronger, and he found work. Within a month, he could go back home to his family.

The salvation of God is near, very near, close as the chill in the air, close as the foggy breath before you, close as the North wind. God is coming to you bursting through a bathroom door, speaking in the voice of a stranger, slipping in through the birth of a baby in a stable, laid in a manger.

The salvation of God is near, very near. Look for the signs, get ready, don't miss it. Prepare your hearts for the birth of God. Be born in us, here and now, today.

Zach and Andie Kubik

In another time, in another place, I pulled into the hospital parking lot. I put out my "clergy" ID sticker on the dash, picked up my prayer book, and rushed inside. The volunteer at the desk told me the floor and room number. It was neonatal intensive care. The babies, twins, a boy and girl, had been born too soon, way too soon. Their mother was still heavily sedated. Their father was with me standing next to their twin incubators, clear plastic bubble-like machines with pumps and wires and tubes, full banks of monitors and lights.

And there in each one was a baby, a little human being no more than eight inches long. Their skin was so thin you could see right through it to every vein and every artery. Their tiny hands were smaller than the nail on your little finger. Yet from each face was a tiny baby respirator, a feeding tube. There were electrodes and wires attached to their chests. And every other second, there seemed to be a breath, in and out, in time with the beeping monitor, a fragile rhythm of life.

I reached through an opening into each incubator and touched the tiny head of each child with a drop of water. I prayed a prayer of blessing; I prayed a prayer of healing and of hope. And my heart broke. I wanted to do something. I wanted to call down a legion of angels to save these two angels from being dashed on the rocks of premature birth. O God, lift up your holy ones and let them live!

A few short days later Andie died. And then a week later Zach died as well. It was over. Two lives, so brief were gone.

9

OTHER ROOMS, OTHER VOICES

By the rivers of Babylon— there we sat down and there we wept when
we remembered Zion. On the willows there we hung up our harps. For
there our captors asked us for songs, and our tormentors asked for
mirth, saying, "Sing us one of the songs of Zion!" How could we sing
the Lord's song in a foreign land?
If I forget you, O Jerusalem, let my righthand wither! Let my tongue
cling to the roof of my mouth, if I do not remember you, if I do not
set Jerusalem above my highest joy. Remember, O Lord, against the
Edomites the day of Jerusalem's fall, how they said, "Tear it down!
Tear it down! Down to its foundations!"
O daughter Babylon, you devastator! Happy shall they be who pay you
back what you have done to us! Happy shall they be who take your
little ones and dash them against the rock!

(PSALM 137, NRSV)

Great Rift Valley

WE LOADED INTO THE CAR, very early before dawn in the cool,
moist air of Nairobi, Kenya. Rev. Dr. Timothy Nyoja, Rev.
Catherine Chalin, and myself were headed to Nakuru, to the

regional courthouse there to attend the trial of a notorious human rights activist, Koige Wa Wameri. He was being tried for the murder of a civil official there in Nakuru, a crime that he could never had committed. As was obvious to the everyone who were familiar with the circumstances of the event, Koige was being framed, set up to take the fall for the murder in order to eliminate him and his human rights battle against the government of the Daniel Arap Moi, president of Kenya.

We three Presbyterian ministers were attending the trial, in order to publicly witness this miscarriage of justice. The drive from Nairobi to Nakuru followed a major highway leading out of the city, going steadily upward, climbing the mountains of central Kenya. Our path wound circuitously through rain forests, rock fields and valleys, following switchbacks along the side of the rising mountain range.

Then at several thousand feet altitude, the rain forest cleared away, and there before us was a vision of the Great Rift Valley. We could see for hundreds of miles in all directions, north and south, east and west. The broad valley was a brown savannah, acacia trees and rivers of grass. Ringed by the mountains of western Kenya, the Abedare National Park on the north, and Masai Mara National Preserve on the south, our eyes followed the central valley, dotted with herds of wildebeest, prominent rock outcrops and occasional lakes and watering holes.

The Great Rift Valley demarcates where several great geological plates are merging together and pulling apart. It stretched almost 5,000 miles, from the Beqaa Valley in Lebanon in the north to Mozambique in the south. It encompasses the Sea of Galilee, the Dead Sea, the gulf of Aqaba, the whole Red Sea, the Afar Valley in Ethiopia, Lake Turkana, Lake Victoria, and Lake Malawi. Here in Kenya, the beauty and grandeur of the Great Rift Valley are on full display.

The road into Nakuru turns away from the valley, inward along the way past Nakuru National Park and Lake Nakuru. The lake is a broad, shallow expanse of water. Flocks of thousands of flamingos fill the lake, creating a moving expanse of pink against

the rippling wind-blown water. We saw Elephants, giraffe, wildebeest and antelope around the edges of the park as we made our
way to the courthouse in the center of town.

A large crowd gathered outside the courthouse which could
hold fewer than a hundred people. The three of us, one African
and two white ministers, put on our clergy robes when we got out
of the car. Catherine and I put on our black robes with red stoles.
Timothy put on a multi-colored, brightly designed robe with African patterns, rainbows and butterflies which had been designed
and made by the women of his congregation.

We entered the courthouse and sat together in front row
center, directly across of the judge's bench. All rose as the judge
was introduced and entered the courthouse. He looked directly at
Timothy and began the trial in earnest. Koige and two co-defen-
dants sat on the left with their lawyers. This was to be a bench trial;
no jury was seated. The prosecution began its case, summarizing
the supposed facts of the case. Several state's witnesses were called
through the morning, and more after a morning break. The de-
fense witnesses who could have given Koige an alibi and exculpa-
tory testimony, were ruled out of order and were not allowed to
testify.

The case did not conclude that day and court was adjourned
until the next day. But from testimony given and rulings from the
bench it was clear that the outcome of the trial was predetermined.
Koige was not going to be given a fair trial. He guilt was preor-
dained and he was facing a probably death sentence.

The judge gaveled the day's proceedings to a close, and then
rose to leave the courtroom. And as he did, before anyone else in
the room moved, Timothy rose from his seat, lifted his arms, and
in a bold declarative voice, said "Let us pray." Silence fell across
the room, No one moved. The judge, the prosecutors, the police
officers who filled the doorways, the lawyers and the defendants
stood motionless. Everyone bowed their heads.

Then Timothy prayed. He prayed for justice in this trial. He
prayed for fairness in the testimony and in the proceedings. He
prayed for the soul of the man who had been murdered. He prayed

that the true perpetrators of the crime might be found. He prayed that the hearts of judge and prosecutors, the police and the president of the Kenya might be opened, that justice and human rights might found in the country of Kenya. He prayed for God's peace and God's justice to rule in the hearts of all Kenyans. He thanked God, and said "Amen." Not a single word was spoken as everyone left the courthouse in silence.

Koige's trial continued for several more days, and ultimately, he was convicted. He was imprisoned for a few years, but later released on appeal.

My time in Kenya was part of a three-month sabbatical from my congregational ministry at Clifton Presbyterian Church in Georgia. One of my duties while in Kenya was to assist in the work of the presbytery of Kikuyu. I preached in several churches including the Church of the Torch in Kikuyu and St. Andrews Presbyterian, a large church in downtown Nairobi. I presided over funerals and participated in church dedication services.

One morning I accompanied the executive presbyter on a visit to a local congregation in a small village next to Kikuyu. We walked from the presbytery office down a wide dirt path past houses and family compounds for about a mile to the next village. Each compound was encircled by stone walls, topped by broken glass for security against thieves and robbers.

As we walked down the path, we came upon a large, charred and burnt area in the middle of the path. Curious, we asked what had caused that unusual burned area. We were told by the local folk accompanying us, that the previous night a thief had been caught breaking into one of the nearby compounds. Rather than turning him into the local police, the community bound the thief, killed him and burned his body in the middle of the path, as a warning to others who would break in and steal.

On another day, I joined a delegation from the presbytery to participate in the dedication service for the opening a new Teacher's School in Rubate on the eastern slope of Mount Kenya. It was an all-day affair taking place on the large outdoor ball field next to the school. There were thousands of people gathered there with clergy from all over Kenya in attendance. When it came time for the service to begin, the clergy gathered in the rear of field, put on their clerical robes and stoles and lined up for a long processional ceremony. I joined the procession and began a slow march through the crowd to the front of the worship area.

About half-way across the field, surrounded by crowds of people singing and dancing, a man rushed forward out of the crowd. He came directly over to me, grabbed my robe and fell on his knees. He was thin, shabbily dressed, virtually only in rags. His hair was ratted and long, scraggy beard. He appeared to be like the many homeless people I worked with back at my home church in Atlanta. He cried out to me, in heavily accented English, "Help me! Oh please, save me!" Again and again, as he dragged on the hem of my robe and I tried to move forward in the clergy processional.

I kept moving with the other clergy, and this man slowly fell away, pushed aside by others in the crowd. We proceed with long and joyous dedication service. Afterward, I searched for this man, hoping to be able to respond to his pleas with some kind of help or assistance, but he was nowhere to be found.

Later, it occurred to me how much this incident resembled what has come to be called the "Triumphal Entry," Palm Sunday in Jesus life. A crowd of people, calling out "Hosanna" which in Aramaic actually means "Save us!" I certainly didn't feel like I was some reincarnation of Jesus that day in Rubate. But perhaps I was a symbol of a rich, white, man of God being called on to "save" these poor Africans. Euro-American paternalism embodied. I was not comfortable with that image.

One day, our family traveled from the church center in Kikuyu to the small township outside the city, not far away. Our car made its way along the single path road, winding and irregular, pocked with potholes and washed away shoulders, through the innumerable small houses and intersections on the outskirts of Nairobi, Kenya.

Along the way, we passed through the commercial district called "Dagoretti." It was just a collection of shacks, thousands of them collected around a few open-air markets, some vegetables, and an open butcher shop. The side streets were all mud with open sewers running down both sides. There were piles and piles of trash and garbage lining the road, some smoldering from open fires. The smell of rotting trash and running sewers was choking.

We crept along through the crowd, windows rolled up tight, trying not to attract the attention of the incessant hands reaching out to the foreigners to buy a trinket or two, or give out a shilling. Our driver stopped however as a small figure darted passed in front of the car. The little girl couldn't have been older than three. She was bare foot, almost naked. Her belly was distended, her hair a brownish-orange, all telltale signs of malnutrition. She had been standing on one of the smoking mounds of trash. I thought she was playing at first, until I realized that her scratching and digging in the mound was a search for food. She looked at us with large blank eyes.

My heart broke as I watched her. I wanted to stop and give her all that I had right then. I wanted to command the stones all around us to be turned into bread. I wanted God to fix it right then there. Feed your hungry children.

10

THE WHOLE PEOPLE OF GOD

A bright light will shine to all the ends of the earth;
many nations will come to you from far away,
the inhabitants of the remotest parts of the earth to your holy name,
bearing gifts in their hands for the King of heaven.
Generation after generation will give joyful praise in you;
the name of the chosen city will endure forever . . .
Happy are those who love you,
and happy are those who rejoice in your prosperity.
Happy also are all people who grieve with you
because of your afflictions;
for they will rejoice with you
and witness all your glory forever.

(TOBIT 13: 11,14; NRSV)

Silver Spring Presbyterian Church

SILVER SPRING PRESBYTERIAN CHURCH (SSPC) was formed in a
suburb of Washington D.C. in 1953. It was part of the great population expansion in the post-war urban areas. And with population
growth came new churches. SSPC grew rapidly in its early years,

expanding from meeting in homes in the location community, to a local high school, to building its own facility, a modern church in the round sanctuary reflecting the aesthetic sensibilities of the mid-1960s neo-modernist theology.

The first permanent pastor of the church was a young liberal, progressive thinker committed to anti-war and civil rights theology. The story goes that he answered the call of Martin Luther King Jr. to come to Selma, Alabama to march across the Edmond Pettus bridge in 1965 along with many other white, liberal church leaders. The Silver Spring Church had grown to over 900 members at that point. But after he marched in Selma, some of the congregation left, and the mostly white congregation shrank to a stable 300–400 members.

SSPC remained an active progressive congregation for many years thereafter. The church welcomed its first non-white members in the early 60's and welcomed its first African members in the mid 80's. A staff member at the Cameroonian embassy in DC was looking for a Presbyterian congregation to join with his young family. They found SSPC responsive to their needs. Many other Cameroonians soon followed as well as Presbyterians from Ghana and Nigeria. By the mid 1990s, over 20% of the congregation was from Africa.

Likewise, by the mid 1990's, SSPC was following a radically inclusive path, welcoming into full membership and ministry members of the gay and lesbian community. The national Presbyterian church was still rejecting that radical inclusion, but SSPC joined the More Light Presbyterian Church (MLP) network in 1995 to resist the national position on gay and lesbian inclusion and work for change in the theological position. The African members of the church were uneasy with SSPC's new decision on inclusion. The African church itself was not accepting of gay Christian ministry and the African members at SSPC found it difficult to welcome gay and lesbian members alongside their own. But they were in a minority in 1995 and could not change the vote to join the MLP network.

I was called to service as pastor of Silver Spring Presbyterian Church in January of 2000. I was excited about serving in a congregation that was fully inclusive of all of God's children, black and white, women and men, adults and children, all cultures and immigrants, and the LGBT community, gay and lesbian Christians. SSPC seems to be the complete embodiment of the Matthew 25 commandment, "In as much as you have done it unto the least of these, my sisters and brothers, you have done it unto me." Silver Spring church was known as the "roundtable church," a church that literally worshipped in a circle around a round-shaped communion table with all members gathered equally around the Eucharist, the holy meal with Jesus.

I began my ministry at SSPC reveling in the wonderful multicolor, multicultural mix of the faithful of all races and cultures, ages, genders and sexual orientations. I extended the invitation to full participation and leadership to everyone regardless of traditional limits and expectations. Africans assumed full leadership on session and church committees.

Worship became an exciting blend of traditional presbyterian hymns and African choruses and choirs. Eventually there were 12 singing groups and choirs, leading worship with voices, processions, drums, clapping and dancing. Gay members provided worship leadership and preaching. Many Sundays over 50 children came forward for the Children's Lesson, as well as reading scripture and leading worship. I have never before experienced a more exciting and spiritually rich worship service.

Consequently, the church began to grow again. When I first came to SSPC, the membership had shrunk to around 180, with an average 75 to 100 in worship each Sunday. Immediately the church began welcoming new members. Each new member class was full to overflowing. Within two years there were over 300 members, by year eight, 400 members. The sanctuary was full to overflowing every Sunday, using the Fellowship Hall for extra seating and a video link to the service. By the time I finally retired at eighteen years, SSPC had over 650 members.

Most of that new membership came from the African immigrant community, the large majority of whom came from Cameroon. When I came to SSPC the membership was about 60% white and 40% black, African and African American. That percentage changed through the years until the congregation was almost 99% of African descent. There was a handful of new members from the white community, but most were immigrants, joining family and friends who likewise had immigrated earlier.

In 2002, I participated in a delegation sent from SSPC to Cameroon to visit with the Presbyterian Church in Cameroon (PCC) and to establish a sister–church relationship with a congregation of the PCC. Five of us on the delegation included two Cameroonians, Lydia Evakise and Esther Mbiakoup, Mildred Fon, an African American woman, and Stanley Bliss, a parish associate of the SSPC who is gay. We visited several congregations in the NW and SW regions of Cameroon. I preached at Bueatown Presbyterian Church, the church which agreed to enter a sister–church relationship with SSPC.

We also consulted with the leadership of the PCC, the moderator Nyansako Ni-Nku, and the presidents of the Christian Women (CWF) and Christian Men's (CMF) Fellowship. We spent a long time with Mrs. Elizabeth Lena Gana, national president of the CWF. She was extraordinarily welcoming and supportive of Cameroonian membership and participation at SSPC. She blessed the formation of a Christian Women Fellowship at SSPC, following the model, patterns and constitution of the CWF in Cameroon. She endorsed the formation of a partnership between the Presbyterian Church (USA) and the PCC, sharing ministry in the fellowship groups, CWF and CMF.

That partnership was soon endorsed by the moderator of the PCC, Nyansako Ni-Nku. The following year, Mrs. Gana visited SSPC to be a part of the dedication of the first CWF group in the USA at Silver Spring church. The women's group started small with just a handful participating, but soon grew exponentially as news of the formation of a real CWF group in the United States spread among the Cameroonian diaspora. Eventually CWF at SSPC grew to over 100 women and CWF groups started in other churches in the PCUSA in Maryland and across the country.

In 2004 a Christian Men's Fellowship (CMF) group started as SSPC as well which likewise led to women's and men's groups forming in other PCUSA churches. But 2004 was also the year that dissent and controversy entered the multicultural life of SSPC. As the CWF were creating their first handbook/constitution for the groups in the USA, the issue of inclusion of homosexual members into the groups came front and center of the conversation. The African community had always been uneasy about SSPC's identity as a More Light Congregation, a church that welcomed the full membership and ministry of LGBT Christians, but that concern had most remained unspoken. Now the issue was brought front and center. How could African Christians worship alongside with equal standing gay and lesbians? Could CWF be a fully inclusive organization or would it leave SSPC completely?

In the meantime, a reporter at The Washington Post had heard that Silver Spring Presbyterian Church was a church that included a large percentage of members who had immigrated from Africa, as well as a great number of gay and lesbian Christians fully accepted into membership and leadership. The Post had also heard that these two communities did not naturally mix. The African church did not normally accept open homosexuals into membership. So, the newspaper sent a reporter to do a profile on this church which included both of these communities. How did they get along? Did the African community reverse its historical rejection of the gay community or did it change its mind and its heart to become fully welcoming of others just as they had been welcomed themselves?

In the course of interviewing many members of SSPC from both communities, the Post reporter was unable to answer either of those questions. The gay community and the immigrant community did get along amicably, but not without some tension and not with full acceptance. The interviews and questions from the reporter brought to the surface feelings and judgements that before had lingered in thoughts but not spoken out loud. Now words were spoken. Rejecting glances were speared across the pews on Sunday morning. The gay community felt open rejection and exclusion.

It wasn't long after the article profiling SSPC appeared on the front page the Sunday morning paper that the LGBT community at Silver Spring began leaving the congregation. Within a year they were mostly gone. Only a handful of loyalists were willing to stick around in an atmosphere of open rejection. Silver Spring remained a "More Light" congregation, but it was inclusive in name only, without the significant presence of gay and lesbian Christians.

Later that year, Mrs. Gana, the national president of CWF (PPC), came to the United States to visit groups in the PCUSA, as well as to receive medical treatment for cancer. I visited her in the hospital here in the DC area as well as in Georgia near where she had family living. Standing by her hospital bed, we talked for a long time about many things. We talked about discipleship, about commitment, about a life of loving and serving God.

We talked about the gospel imperative to share the good news of God in Jesus Christ, to share the love of God in Christ. Mostly she spoke passionately about her faith in Jesus Christ. It was all consuming for her. The cancer had metastasized to her brain by then. She was in almost constant pain, and she knew that she was entering her last days. As she talked about God, it appeared as if her countenance actually glowed. She was radiant. We prayed together, not for healing or recovery into a long life. We prayed rather for God's presence and God's peace in this moment of dying. And I am convinced that as she did pass from this world just a week later, she was united with God in death, just as she had been in life.

Thin Places

Marsha and I were sitting on the edge of a cliff, looking down at the beach a few yards below us, the great sea waves crashing against the rocks and the sand. Behind us was a long, grassy meadow, some sheep and cattle grazing, with rock outcrops and trees here and there. Still further to the south was the great Abbey, the ancient monastery church which lay in ruins for many centuries, and now is rebuilt and center of worship and is still a place of holiness and spirit.

We were on Iona, a small island off the west coast of Scotland. More than pretty or picturesque, Iona is place referred to by Celtic Christians, as a "thin place." A thin place. It is place where the distance between heaven and earth appears to have become very small. Thin. A place where the ordinary and the holy overlap. Thin places are where the earthbound veil momentarily lifts and we behold God, experience the presence of the one in whom we live all the time anyway, a special place where God lives.

On Iona, we felt that special presence of God. It is a place permeable with the divine. I feel that same way about other places in the world. The wilderness of northern New Mexico, near the Presbyterian Conference center called Ghost Ranch. I have gone hiking there and gone on spiritual retreat there. The big blue sky, the high desert mesas, the pinion pine and junipers trees, the sculpted arroyos, soaring hawks, scampering lizards, the afternoon storms, the blistering noonday sun, it all combined to feel like a thin place, a place where God lives, a holy place.

Each year our family goes on holiday at the beach. The crashing waves, the sun the sand, the limitless sky, the wind in my face, the water on my body, it all calls me into the presence of God, the nourishing, rejuvenating, transforming presence of God.

Each of these places are holy places, places to find the presence of God.

There is an island off the coast of Ireland, called Skellig Michael. It is a tiny island, only a few hundred meters around, but it is very tall and pointed. There is no coast line to it, only a rocky wall rising right up out of the ocean to a height of almost seven hundred feet. Visitors must climb by way of a narrow rocky path that winds around until they reached the pointed top.

Seventeen hundred years ago, a small band of monks climbed Skellig Michael and built a small monastery at the very top. And there they lived, alone and isolated, generation after generation, for hundreds of years, worshipping and praying, maintaining a holy presence alone against the rest of the world.

The rocky ruins of that monastery are still there. A few years ago, I wanted to visit that island and experience the remains of that holy place. The island is about ten miles off the coast of Ireland and the only way to get there is by small boat. The waters in between are rough and choppy. Early one morning, Marsha and I got into our boat with about 20 other visitors. We put on our rain ponchos to protect us from the saltwater spray, and headed out into rough water.

Up and down, up and down, up and down, we bounced on the choppy waves. It wasn't long however before I was seeing green—not the greenery of coastal forests, but the green of sea sickness. I don't know how many of you have experienced seasickness, but it is one the worst forms of nausea possible, stomach roiling, fevered brow, the was whole world spinning.

About half way across the waters I remembered an old seasickness remedy I had heard about a while before. Instead of holding your head down between your legs, you rise up and look across the horizon. Find a stable landmark, a mountain, a hill, and focus on that fixed point. Hold your gaze firmly on that fixed point. While the boat is bouncing all over, look at that mountain, keep your eyes on the goal of you traveling, and the sickness of the present will subside.

So, I rose up, and immediately I saw the pointed outcrop of Skellig Michael on the horizon. I fixed my gaze on the top of the island mountain, and soon my sickness passed. I made it through the choppy waters in peace. Perhaps this is a metaphor for the way to navigate through the choppy waters of life. Instead of burying your head and your heart in the rough waters of life, the way to get through is to focus on the long view, the big picture, the stable destination on the far horizon. Maybe this is the way to make it through.

A Vigil with Death

Reflecting on eighteen years of ministry at SSPC, I realize that I was driven by an overwhelming vision of the "Whole People of God." I had a passion for a church that included all people of the earth, all races, all nationalities, all cultures serving God together equally as men and women, old and young, gay and straight. One church, one body, one faith, one Lord and Savior Jesus Christ. My greatest desire was to welcome all people to worship together, breaking down all barriers that separate us. And inviting everyone to serve God as equal children of God together.

I invited everyone to bring their special gifts to God in worship, singing in new choirs, dancing, clapping and shouting in new groups, praising God together. We welcomed spontaneity in worship, changing the order of worship as the Spirit moved, offering free form prayers and songs, sharing drums, praise band instruments, solo offerings, songs from our grandmas, songs in French, Douala, Mangaka, Twi and other languages of the earth. I invited new leadership in the governing bodies of the church, giving all voices a say in the life of the church. I preached a message of welcome and inclusion, a word of Good News to everyone regardless of where they came from.

But as often as I was called on to give a message of new life in service to a living God, I was also called on to give witness to the presence of God in the moments of suffering and in final passage of death. Hospital visits, sick visits, wake keepings, visitations, funerals and death vigils were as much a part of my ministry at SSPC as anything else I did. Witnessing to the holiness of the ubiquity of suffering and universal process of dying was the defining mark of my ministry.

In the long ministry at SSPC, I prayed and preached at over 140 wake-keeping services, 84 funerals and memorial services, and countless hospital visits for people suffering and some who ultimately died. Many of these services involved standing by the bedside of the dying as they took their last breaths and standing in vigil beside the dead body of a beloved member of the body of Christ frozen in the emptiness of death. Giving witness in the presence of suffering and death punctuated every movement in ministry at SSPC.

Polly Chirieleison was the first member of SSPC to die after I began my ministry there. Shortly following was Matilda Mays, Chet Benjamin, Mary K. Register and Jean McGregor. All were long-time members, white members of the church: liberal, progressive, and inclusive minded. Jean was an open lesbian member who had been in a long-term partnership. Next came Luke Fon, son of a Cameroonian tribal chief and married to an African American elder and church leader, Mildred Fon. Gerry Flores was a Hispanic member and part of the Pastoral Nominating Committee that called me to SSPC. He died in 2002.

Warren McCawley died in 2003 after suffering a stroke and being sustained on a breathing machine for six months. Greg Mayfield was an African American and leader of the active and vibrant youth group at SSPC. He died in 2004 succumbing to AIDS/HIV.

Peter Njang was a new immigrant from Cameroon in 2004. He had been in this country for only two weeks and was living with his uncle's family who were members of SSPC. One afternoon he was returning to the apartment after running some errands around town. He had forgotten his key to the apartment and could not get in. He walked around to the back window of the apartment to get the attention of someone within.

A police cruiser was passing through the parking lot and noticed a black man around the windows of the building. The two officers got out of the car and called over to the man. Peter walked over and tried to explain his dilemma. When he reached for his identification from his pocket, the officers drew their weapons and shot him. The officers said that he had a box cutter and was threatening to attack them. No box cutter was ever found. Njang died instantly. No police officer was ever disciplined or held accountable for Peter's death.

Mary A. Register, Mary K.'s mother, also died in 2004 after a long lingering illness. Rose Bolima was killed in an auto accident while visiting home in Cameroon. Bob Parkinson, Jessie Kirk and

Ruby Stark, long-time members, died in 2005. Bob Cantrell was the church treasurer for 18 years, and died in 2006. Pete Vial was also a longtime member of the church who had contracted MS and had used a wheelchair for most of his adult life. He died in 2007.

Mark Karis was a young man in his forties when he died of cancer. Howard Griffin was only in his twenties when he died in an auto accident. Mimi Josiane Banga was a new immigrant from francophone Cameroon, likewise in her twenties. She died from HIV/AIDS. Her husband, Ferdinand, died a few years later. Three young children, Chanelle, Megan, and Mackenzie Foncham, died horribly in a house fire in June of that year.

Flo Hill

Flo Hill was a much-loved elder, leader and teacher in the congregation. She was a retired registered nurse. She was the first female elected elder at 6th Presbyterian Church in Pittsburgh. She served as an elder on session several times at Silver Spring Presbyterian Church. She was elected to serve as a commissioner to the national General Assembly of the PC(USA).

At SSPC, Flo was committed to Christian Education, organizing and building our Sunday School program. She loved children of all ages and always sought to nurture their spiritual growth. She loved and was especially creative in doing crafts for at Christmas for Advent and for Vacation Bible School. She taught and sustained the Adult Lectionary Class, meeting every Sunday morning, studying the Bible lessons for that week. Flo loved to wrestle with every text, probing for the deeper meaning and resonance. She often wrote her own commentaries on the Bible passages.

She especially liked to write Midrash—an extended commentary on the text filling out the meaning of just a few lines. She would take on the voice of a Bible character and imagine what they were thinking or feeling: Lazarus, Jonah, the prodigal son, or the older brother. She gave voice to the women of scripture: the woman at the well, Mary and Martha, the Canaanite woman, Shiphrah and Puah, the midwives of Egypt. She gave them life and depth.

Flo was a theologian—although she would never claim the title—the finest lay theologian I have ever known. She wrote the daily devotional guides for our congregation for Lent and Advent for many years. For the last two years she wrote the "Daily Grace for Living" the daily devotional that was in our service bulletin every Sunday for the upcoming week. Each one is a jewel of wisdom, insight and compassion. She taught many classes. Flo preached in the SSPC pulpit.

Flo was also committed to mission and service. She was a regular volunteer in church mission outreach. She led the congregation in becoming an open and affirming church, a More Light Church, open to the membership and ministry of gay and lesbian Christians. She led the church in being open to all races and cultures, helping us to become a multiracial, multicultural church. She loved the blending of cultures at SSPC.

Her mission commitment grew beyond this congregation alone. She was one of the founders and the chair of the Board of MUSST, Ministries United Silver Spring Takoma Park. She volunteered there every week. Hundreds of families were helped with medical bills and threatened evictions because of Flo's efforts.

Flo was also committed to the spiritual growth of the congregation. She encouraged the formation of prayer groups and special classes on spiritual formation and prayer. She coordinated the "prayer chain" of the church through which anyone could request prayer and then know that they were prayed for by members of the church. Flo helped begin the services of healing and wholeness within the church.

Flo was a voracious reader. She read the NY Times every day, multiple magazines, like the New Yorker and Harpers. She would often cut out articles that she thought I would be interested in (issues of religion, science, politics) and we would discuss them. She read more books in a week than I could read in a year—heavy theological books, novels, and even what she called "flippies," light reading just for fun.

She loved to go to the movies and we would often discuss the latest blockbuster or the most obscure art film in town. She loved music, concerts and live performances of drama.

Flo was a painter. The walls of her home are graced by many of her abstract paintings. Her paintings show beauty, movement, passion and fire. I particularly love her painting called "The Butterfly Man." It is a figure made up all of butterfly wings all fluttering against a red background that give the impression of life and fire.

Flo was also a poet. She wrote hundreds of poems, some about serious issues of life and death, some about relationships with family and friends, some about theological issues, even about the liturgical year—Advent, Lent, Easter, and Ordinary time. She wrote about flowers in the spring, snow in winter, about growing up, about raising children, about making cookies for the neighborhood kids. She wrote about strong feelings, love, joy, anger, fear. She wrote about the ordinary and the extraordinary. She wrote about life.

The "hard cold reality" (as Flo often like to say) is that in all of her life, through all of her life, and beyond her life, Flo loved God-with all her heart, mind, strength and soul, and she loved her neighbor with equal parts of her being.

She loved. And God's love lived in her.

I stood regular vigil by Flo's bedside as she bore the pain and suffering of pancreatic cancer the last ten months of her life. She died peacefully at home in bed in June of 2007.

In February of 2008 Jacques Tchouante died suddenly of a heart attack. Three months later his daughter, Jeannie died of metastatic breast cancer leaving behind a newborn infant. Betty Smith was the oldest member of SSPC, a retired nurse of over forty years, died at age 93. Another longtime member, Cathy Crosby died in 2011, along with Helen Melaney, Lucas Atongnong and Helen Ngam. In contrast, Edith Ngang was only 19 when she died suddenly of a congenital heart defect. Fritz Lotonga was in his forties when he died of HIV/AIDS. Dorothy Forbai died of cancer that same year.

Anastasia Ade was one of the founding members of Christian Women Fellowship at SSPC. She had joined CWF in Cameroon when she was a young mother and new Presbyterian. In the USA, she was the matriarch of the large Ade family, seven children and many grandchildren, all of whom were active members of the church. Her husband was Esau Ade who had been an Olympic runner for Cameroon and was now a founding member of Christian Men Fellowship. Anastasia was in many ways the matriarch of the whole congregation. She led the church by her strong faith, boundless courage, effervescent spirit, and deep wisdom.

In the CWF, she was not the president of the groups, but she was the wise one who all the presidents went to for counsel and support. Her favorite CWF chorus was a song that expressed her faithful vision of Christian discipleship:

Bend low, bend low, bend low, bend low bend low

And see what the Lord can do (everybody bend low) [repeat]

Moses in the wilderness, Moses in the wilderness

He bends low and talks to God, and the power of the Lord comes through (chorus)

Daniel in the lion's den, Daniel in the lion's den

He bends low and talks to God and the power of the Lord comes through (chorus)

Jesus in the wilderness, Jesus in the wilderness

He bends low and talks to God and the power of the Lord comes through (chorus)

One day in 2012 while driving back to her home in Washington, DC, Anastasia suffered a massive stroke and crashed her car into the roadside. She was rushed to the nearest hospital and treated in the critical care unit. Her whole family held vigil around her bed for over a week, but she never regained consciousness. I also stood next to her and prayed and sang her favorite chorus when the decision to remove life support was made. She died a few hours later.

In the early hours of the morning in September of 2012, I received a call from Bridget Asana informing me that her husband, Gustav, who had also recently suffered stroke, was near death in the intensive care ward of a different hospital. I rushed to his bed side, and along with other CWF and CMF members and his whole family, we prayed and sang songs for healing and recovery. But his injury was too severe for recovery. Gustav Asana died a few hours later.

In 2013, Ngoh Forchick Tekwe, a young man of not yet 19 years, suddenly downed in the waters of the Potomac River after wading of the shore of the Billy Goat Trail in Great Falls National Park near D.C. They found his body the next day stuck in a sink hole in the river.

In 2014, Vincent Manjo, like so many others in the African community, suffered a massive stroke. After initial treatment, he was remained unconscious and sustained on life support in a nursing home for over eight months before he died.

Bill Stockton was a longtime member of SSPC. His family, his wife Irma, and children became a part of the community fifty years before. Bill was a retired psychoanalyst and a thoughtful and committed Christian who reveled in the engagement of deep theological discussions and critical thought. He also loved music and was a very talented singer. He was a loyal member of the Chancel Choir and often sang powerfully and moving solos on special occasions. On Christmas Eve every year, he sang "O Holy Night", moving everyone to tears.

Bill had a heart attack in 2014. Hospitalized, there was some debate as to whether he was strong enough to survive the needed heart by-pass surgery. Ultimately the surgery proceeded, but his strength never returned. Day by day, he grew weaker and it became clear he would not survive the trauma of the by-pass surgery. With his family and other SSPC friends, we stood around his bed and prayed and sang songs of the hope and healing, songs praising God's loving care and presence.

On my last visit to his hospital room, I prayed a special prayer of hope and healing and I bent over to give him a final hug. With that, he stretched up and kissed me on the cheek and said "thank you." A few days later, at a recovery center nearby, Bill Stockton passed away quietly in his sleep.

John Hoffsommer was a long-time member of SSPC. He served God in this congregation for over fifty years along with his wife, Becky and two children, Cynthia and Heather. Becky passed away early in life suffering from leukemia in 1995. John was a faithful elder at SSPC, serving on many committees, serving in mission in the community. He was the first chair of the reconstituted Board of deacons. He was the co-chair of the pastor nominating committee that called me as pastor to Silver Spring Church.

John was also a very talented musician. He sang in the Chancel Choir; he organized and played in the Bell choir. But his greatest passion was playing the piano. He gave many concerts. He played duets with many friends. He accompanied the children's choir at SSPC, and played many special music offerings in worship. His touch at the piano was lyrical, sensitive and beautiful.

In one particular service at SSPC, John played the offertory music. The piece he played was "Moderato cantabile" by Dennis Alexander. John's interpretation was stunning. It was breathtaking, one of the most beautiful, worshipful musical offerings I have ever heard. Afterward, John returned to his seat, and a few moments later, he collapsed with a heart attack. Everything in worship stopped and members began to pray and to sing softly. Medical professionals in the congregation quickly gathered around him and administered artificial respiration, keeping him alive until the EMTs arrived to rush him to the hospital. John survived. He lived six more years--six more years of living, loving and laughing, singing and serving, loving God with his whole heart.

Fourteen members of the congregation died in 2014 through 2016. Some were longtime members, some were new immigrants, white members and African members. Another 14 members died in 2017 alone, again some longtime members and some new arrivals. Martin Nchotaku, a young man in his early twenties, was murdered by an ostensive friend in the middle of some kind of transaction that was never fully explained. Jo Crichton died after over fifty years of faithful service at SSPC.

I was engaged in ministry at Silver Spring Presbyterian Church for almost exactly eighteen years to the day. From the very first day until the last, it was a very rich and fulfilling, challenging and rewarding, energizing and exhaustive spiritual experience. But the journey was not easy. There were times of great struggle and conflict. There was the struggle between the gay and the African community. There was some anger and alienation between and white and the African community. There was conflict and struggle within the African community itself, fighting over leadership and power, over theology, church structure and church order. There was jealousy and petty recriminations. There was church splits and betrayals. There was a struggle with church finances, and even criminal embezzlement of church funds.

But through it all, my one vision and purpose as the pastor of this church was to love God, and to love and nurture the whole people of God, to love and serve each member of this community with all my heart, mind, soul and strength. In the end I think I can say I have done that.

A Life Changed Once Again

The overwhelming majority of the Africans at Silver Spring Presbyterian Church were Cameroonians from the English speaking or Anglophone provinces of Cameroon. Although they represented dozens of different tribes and spoke just as many tribal languages, the legacy of colonialism meant that they all spoke and understood English. Conducting worship services in English therefore promoted unity and understanding in this diverse community.

But there were always a significant minority in the congregation who were from the French-speaking provinces of Cameroon, whose understanding of English was rudimentary or barely functional. They came to the English-speaking worship service, but never felt comfortable or at home.

As a way to be of service to this francophone community, the session of SSPC established a French-speaking worship service in 2011. The service took place on Sunday afternoons and was led by the francophone members themselves. French choirs were established. At first French speaking elders did the preaching, but soon a French speaking pastor living in the community was brought in to preach on a regular basis.

This new service worked well for a while afterward. Attendance at the service grew steadily. Other French-speaking Africans from around the Silver Spring community began attending the service, finding for the first time a comfortable spiritually enriching place to worship. But about a year later, the visiting pastor who was preaching the service decided that he wanted to make the francophone service into his own separate congregation. He left the service starting a new church in a building across town, taking about half the French-speaking SSPC members with him.

As a way to avoid repeating such a split again, SSPC engaged a partnership with the Francophone presbyterian Church of Cameroon, the "Eglise Evangelique Camerounaise" (EEC), to provide a guest preacher for the French speaking service at SSPC. The EEC released one of its pastors in Cameroon to come to America and serve as preacher for this service at SSPC.

After some negotiating, VISA applications, and some time in preparation, the French speaking pastor arrived at SSPC. The Rev. Justin Njikeu came to Silver Spring, and at first lived with a member of the congregation. While he still lived there, I went to his apartment for lunch one day, to meet him, get to know him and prepare him for the task ahead.

While driving back to the office from this lunchtime meeting, I received a call that would change my life forever. Nothing would ever be the same--my life, my ministry, my family, my faith, my passions and my sense of trust and safety, nothing would ever be the same.

My son in law, Tim, called to tell me that my grandson, ten-month-old Charles Currie Guzewicz, was dead. Hannah had left him with a baby sitter for a few hours while she ran some errands around town. The sitter put C.C. down for his morning nap as usual. But when he didn't wake up after about an hour of sleeping, she went to his room and found him burning up with fever and not breathing. She tried to revive him and called the EMTs. They arrived a few minutes later and also tried to revive him. Their attempts at artificial resuscitation left C.C. beaten and bruised. He was pronounced dead later at the hospital.

Subsequent testing showed that he was the victim of an acute viral infection called R.S.V., Respiratory Syncytial Virus. RSV is a common respiratory virus that usually causes mild, cold-like symptoms. Most people recover within a week. But it can be deadly in infants and older adults. A fever rages out of control and can stop breathing.

C.C. was the first-born son of our daughter, Hannah and her husband, Tim. They were living in southern Pennsylvania at the time of her pregnancy, just a few hours from us in suburban Maryland. Marsha, my wife, is a very experienced nurse midwife, on staff at George Washington University Hospital as a faculty midwife in DC. Hannah and Tim decided that they wanted Marsha to do the delivery of their first child. So, when Hannah got within days of her delivery due date, they traveled to our home in Maryland to await the onset of labor.

And labor did begin, somewhat earlier than expected, in the middle of the night in our home. By the time Hannah was truly aware of what was happening and could alert Marsha that it was beginning, it was too late to make a run to the hospital. C.C. was born in the early hours of the morning of June 22nd. And so, just like his mother before him, C.C. was born at home attended by a midwife (his grandmother), surrounded by his father and loving friends.

After receiving the call from Tim, I returned back to the office. The shock of the news turned to uncontrollable grief. I fell to the floor of the church hallway and cried. Later, Marsha and I held each other and cried, deep and heartbroken wails and sobs. Immediately we travelled up to Pennsylvania to gather close to Hannah and Tim. By then the house was beginning to fill with family and friends to support them in their grief. Hannah was in bed, completely overcome with desperate sorrow, calling again and again for her baby, her baby who she could not see or hold.

For many hours, Hannah was inconsolable. Her tears and wails went on through the night. Her cries echoed the cries of the mothers of Bethlehem after the slaughter of the innocents: "A voice is heard in Ramah, weeping and great mourning, Rachel weeping for her children and refusing to be comforted, because they are no more." (Matt. 2:17–18). My heart was broken a second time as I witnessed my own baby, my own dear child, suffer such uncontrollable grief.

We all began to get very worried about Hannah. Her grief had become hysterical, out of control. We made the decision to take her to the emergency room to see a doctor for sedation. We had a long wait in the ER, and a longer wait to see a doctor, but finally she received some care and the necessary relief to calm her. She stayed at the hospital overnight and came back home the next day to face the absence of C.C. and the emptiness of loss.

A few days later, I was given the horrible task, along with Tim's father Charlie, of meeting with the funeral home to plan for the rites of C.C.'s passing and to select an appropriate urn to receive his ashes. To select an urn for my grandson's ashes was unthinkable.

And then a day was selected for the final viewing of the body. On the day of the viewing, we all made our way to the funeral home. We were ushered to the room set aside for viewing. A few chairs were there for those who needed to sit, and there at the end of the room, next to a window, was the platform to hold the tiny body of our grandson. He was dressed in a nice shirt pants and shoes. His eyes were closed, face translucent white. Cold to the touch. We all stood by him, at first in utter silence, and then in muffled tears.

I tried to think of something to say. I am a minister. I am supposed to have words for occasions like this. After forty years of ministry, I have stood next to many dead bodies. I have been present when the last breath of life is taken. I have preached many funeral sermons with a casket right before me. My very first act of ministry I believe was at seventeen-years-old, standing next the body of my grandfather, C.C. Burris, and offering a prayer for his memory and a prayer of his blessing.

And here I was, standing next to the body of my grandson, C.C. Guzewicz. I tried to say something appropriate, something comforting, something pastoral, but nothing would come. I tried to say a prayer. I may have said a prayer but I don't remember anything said. I had nothing. Just an empty yawning hole of grief. That's all there was.

11

THE SUFFERING OF GOD

But Moses implored the LORD his God, and said, "O LORD, why does your wrath burn hot against your people, whom you brought out of the land of Egypt with great power and with a mighty hand? [12] Why should the Egyptians say, 'It was with evil intent that he brought them out to kill them in the mountains, and to consume them from the face of the earth'? Turn from your fierce wrath; change your mind and do not bring disaster on your people. [13] Remember Abraham, Isaac, and Israel, your servants, how you swore to them by your own self, saying to them, 'I will multiply your descendants like the stars of heaven, and all this land that I have promised I will give to your descendants, and they shall inherit it forever.'" [14] And the LORD changed his mind about the disaster (evil) that he planned to bring on his people.

(EXODUS 32: 11–14, NRSV)

THEODICY IS A BRANCH of systematic theology that deals with the issue of evil and suffering in the light of the existence of an all-good and all-powerful God. If God is loving and omnipotent, where does evil come from? Why does God allow creation to suffer? Theodicy tries to address this unsolvable paradox by defending the holiness and justness of God in spite of the suffering of God's creation.

Both physical and moral evil have been an ever-present part of creation from the very beginning. Suffering is an unrelenting and pervasive dimension of life in all its forms and in all its stages. Suffering in many ways actually defines every moment of life. How did an all-just God create a world full of the persistence of evil? And how did an all-loving God not only permit the existence of suffering but actually seem to will the pervasiveness of suffering in every life?

There have been many attempts to solve this paradox, to explain this apparent contradiction in the character and purpose of God. Some theologians suggest that God did not create evil and suffering but rather that suffering is an after-effect of the movement from universality to particularity. Eternal God is good and loving and perfect. Individual life and particular existence is broken, subject to evil, and defined by suffering: original sin, as it were.

Other theologians have suggested that our understanding of omnipotence is flawed. God is all-powerful and as creator is the source of every moment of existence. But in that omnipotence, God self-limits that power in order to permit creation the freedom to choose good or evil, to choose the holy perfection of God or embrace evil and its concomitant suffering. The evil and suffering we bear as human beings is sourced in our rebellion against God.

Still other theologians have clearly confessed that there is a contradiction between an all-loving God and an all-powerful God. God cannot love perfectly all of creation and at the same time be the omnipotent creator of a world that includes evil and suffering. Our understanding of omnipotence is not just flawed, it is wrong. We must choose either an all-loving God or an all-powerful God. An all-loving God is good. An all-powerful God is a monster. Choosing the monster is unthinkable. Therefore, God is holy and all loving, but God is not all powerful. God did not create evil and suffering. Where did they come from? We don't know; it is a mystery, but they didn't come from God.

This solution creates a kind of ontological dualism, two over-lapping universes, one good and one evil. But such theological Gnosticism is preferable to singular universe that actually wills pervasive evil and suffering. We cannot accept a God who actually is the source of evil and who wills that all human beings suffer.

But what if the solution to the paradox of theodicy were something entirely different? What if the solution was to accept that the paradox of theodicy was no paradox at all? The two contradictory ideas, omnipotence and divine compassion, are perceived as contradictory because we say that they are. We cannot accept the idea of a God who is the source of evil and suffering.

But our scientific understanding of the ongoing creation and function of existence as well as the biblical theological description of the creation and the dynamics of life, both demonstrate that evil and suffering are real and persistent. And theologically we trust that God is good and all loving. Both realities are true. They cannot be contradictory.

We don't have to change our understanding of the omnipotence of God. We do have to change our understanding of the holiness and love of God. God is the source of evil and suffering in the world. And God loves us unconditionally. Both are true. How can we live with that?

Scientifically, our current understanding of how the universe was formed is not that it gently emerged as something out of nothing. Instead, the universe emerged explosively, from an infinitely small singularity in a violently expansive moment, colloquially known as "the Big Bang," into a universe of billions and stars and galaxies. The formation of every star system was made out of explosive upheavals and violent collisions. The stars, planets, galaxies, the visual and unseen universe is the result violent upheaval. The universe is born, in a scientific sense, out of suffering.

Our planet Earth was formed in the collision of star dust and random particles, pulled together by gravity and spun eternally around our fiery star called the Sun. Its early years were dominated by volcanic outbursts all around the planet which ultimately resulted in land masses and oceans. Continents and mountain ranges were formed by the collision of tectonic plates which are grinding together and pulling apart. New lands and masses are forming violently every day.

Life emerged on earth, not with a gentle whimper, but with a violent struggle to survive, to persist, to grow, change and prosper. Every form of life on this planet survives by killing and consuming some other form of life. Nothing lives by only consuming inanimate things. From the smallest protozoa to multi-celled creatures, from insect, plants, to the highest form of animals, all survive by the death and consumption of other living things. Life is sustained and continues by suffering.

The biblical story of creation begins as the Spirit of God hovers over the empty, dark and formless chaos of the deep. God speaks the world into existence. We often imagine this first word of God as calm whisper-like utterance. But I imagine this word from the infinite God as more of an earsplitting roar with tones and timbrels beyond human capacity to hear. The creation of the world would require nothing less. Human life begins when God breathes into hand-formed clay, not with a gentle kiss, but with a blow that imports a soul and supports everyday life for a hundred years.

From that moment on, God interacts with human existence in ways that calls forth work, labor, struggle and ultimately death. From the moment of our first breath, we are fated to work, struggle, suffer and finally to die. No one can avoid it. This is the life God created for us.

God drove Adam and Eve from paradise and sentenced them to a life of work and new babies to be born of labor and pain. The first-born son, Cain, murdered his only brother in a struggle over his offerings that God rejected. A few generations later, the story of Noah proceeds as God initiates the death of almost all of humanity. The rainbow over Arahat is not a sign of God's promise, but a marker of the greatest mass murder in history.

Several generations later, the first patriarch, Abraham, was driven into Egypt by a famine in the land. There the Lord afflicted terrible diseases upon the Egyptians because of their unknown attentions to Abraham's wife, Serah. Later, God again commits mass execution of the entire cities of Sodom and Gomorrah. After granting Abraham the birth of a son through his wife Sarah, God orders Abraham to kill that same son to demonstrate his faithfulness, committing murder to show religious fealty.

Years later, the sons of Jacob slaughter all the males of the Shechemites in revenge for the rape of their sister, Dinah., another mass murder sanctioned by God. Those same brothers soon sell their own brother, Joseph into slavery in Egypt. One of Jacob's sons, Judah, had a son named Er. God killed him because he was perceived as evil. Then God killed Er's brother, Onan, for failing to sleep with his own brother's wife.

Joseph thrives in Egypt. But after all the Hebrews follow him to live in Egypt during a famine, the Hebrews are enslaved by the Egyptians. And they live in slavery for hundreds of years, abandoned by their God. Moses is miraculously saved from the slaughter of all the Hebrew males children by Pharoah. But later he flees from Egypt after he himself murders an Egyptian soldier. Forty years later, Moses returns to free the Hebrews from slavery. He is successful after God again murders all the first-born males of Egypt. The sign of blood marked over the doorways in Passover is as much a sign of divine homicide as it is liberation.

Shortly thereafter, the parted waters of the Red Sea are released to swallow up hundreds of Pharoah's soldiers. Final liberation of the Hebrews is achieved when God kills the Egyptian army. But this is followed by still more slaughter on the way to the Promised land. After it is revealed that the Hebrews began worshipping the Golden calf, God planned to kill all the Hebrew people in anger. But God changed his mind about that evil planned against them. Instead, 3,000 Hebrews were killed in punishment for their evil conduct, and then God brought a plague upon the people to kill even more.

The whole biblical story, from the creation of the world through the Exodus from Egypt to the Promised land has become the template for the pattern of God's interaction with creation. Existence emerges by God's creative action in a dramatic convulsion of something from nothing. Human life rebels against God's omnipotence in an urgent press of particularity over divine transcendence. God responds with a moment-to-moment ontologically-shaped persistence of suffering and finally, death. Liberation, freedom, salvation and new life is purchased with the price of suffering and death.

The incarnation of God in the life, ministry, suffering and death of Jesus Christ is the particular expression of God's emergent creation of the world. The life and finally the crucifixion of Jesus is the perfect expression of immanent creation, singular existence emerging out of the universal divine. The example of Jesus shows us how life is lived. God is embodied finally and completely in suffering and death.

The story of birth of Jesus is surrounded in scandal, hardship, suffering and horrific death. Mary's pregnancy scandalizes the community and threatens even her life. She could have been stoned for conceiving a child out of wedlock. Joseph and Mary's forced travel on the eve of the child's birth brought incredible hardship. The lack of accommodation in Bethlehem was equally difficult. And then, they were forced flee Judea to escape Herod's murderous rampage. Bethlehem was literally bathed in blood shortly after Jesus' birth.

The young family were actually refugees for several years until they could return back to Nazareth. Jesus' younger years may have been relatively peaceful. But in all likelihood those years brought considerable struggle, just to survive given the unexplained absence of Joseph to provide a living for a wife and several children.

Jesus' ministry starts when he reaches adulthood, but it begins with opposition, threats and controversy. After his first sermon in the synagogue of Nazareth, an angry crowd drives him to the brow of a hill and almost throws him over. At every stage in his ministry thereafter the tremendous support he receives from the crowd in towns and villages in Galilee is countered growing opposition from the religious authorities and sectarian leaders. As much as he was loved by the newly faithful, he was hated and despised by just as many.

On the last week of his life, the triumphal entry into Jerusalem is often characterized as a festive celebration of the arrival of the messiah into the holy city. It was, however, anything but. The crowd that day were desperately crying out to be saved from their suffering and their pain while surrounded by others crying out for Jesus' rejection and his blood. The entry was not a party; it was a riot.

And that riotous opposition followed him that week as he taught in the streets of Jerusalem, as he violently cleansed the money-changers and thieves from the Temple, and as he was betrayed and then violently arrested in the Garden of Gethsemane in the dark of night. But that night's violence was only the beginning of what would be the worse suffering anyone could ever imagine.

With the arrest of Jesus, he was brought, bound, and dragged for examination before the religious authorities. He was completely humiliated. He was tried by the Roman authorities before a screaming, blood–thirsty mob. And then was stripped and whipped by the Roman guards until his skin was ripped from his flesh. The pain must have been blinding. He was forced to carry his heavy cross through the streets of Jerusalem until he totally collapsed under its weight.

At the site of crucifixion, his hands and feet were nailed to the wooden cross. Naked, he was lifted up high to hang, bleeding and suffocating by the weight of his own body. For hours he alternately gasped desperately for breath, and passing out from the horrendous pain from the wounds. The only mercy given that day was that his side was pierced by a long spear to hasten his inevitable death so that he would die before sabbath began rather than linger for days.

The suffering and death of Jesus on the cross could easily be said to be the worst pain and suffering that anyone has ever experienced. It crosses the line beyond which pain and suffering loses a scale on which it can be measured. It is total pain, total suffering. In a very real way, the cross recapitulates and encapsulates the pain and suffering of every human being before and after. The cross stands for the suffering of all of us.

Mary, the women and the disciples who stood before the cross that day, witnessed greatest trauma anyone could ever experience. And as such, they were inflicted by the trauma as well. They witnessed and experienced searing psychic, emotional and physical trauma. They were enveloped in horror beyond imagining. And it changed them forever. Every moment, every day, for the rest of their lives they would relive those hours kneeling at the foot of the cross. They would relive every gasp for breath, every cry out in pain, every drop of blood, every twist of sweat.

For the women and the disciples, the visage of the crucifixion became the true substance of faith. To believe in Jesus was to relive the horror of his death. To live in faith is to embrace post-traumatic horror.

That's the way it is with every Christian since that day of crucifixion. We intentionally read or hear preached the gospel accounts the suffering and death of Jesus. We imagine what it was like to be there at the foot of the cross. We identify with Mary and the disciples. We experience the horror for ourselves. And we enter the deep grieving process of watching the suffering and death of someone who we love and who loves us so completely.

This is exactly what happened to me, the seven-year-old boy sitting by himself at a revival meeting when he walked down the aisle in response to the preacher's altar call. I entered into the traumatic grieving process, accepting this as the mark of God's life in the world with us, and resolving to give witness to that truth for the rest of my life. My ministry has been and will always be a witness to the suffering of God.

Christian faith is born at the foot of the cross. It is not the fruit of a transactional analysis of the price paid for sins and the innocence of the one who pays. Faith doesn't not emerge from substitutionary atonement. It doesn't grow out of Jesus' moral example. It is not the result of a ransom paid for out sinful souls. It is not Jesus' defeat of evil, for surely evil was not defeated on the cross. Evil won. Jesus' death did not somehow satisfy God's need for justice. There was no justice on the cross.

It is often said that on the cross, Jesus paid the price for our sins for us. We are all guilty of sin and a price must be paid for those sins. That price is death. But God in Christ chose to pay the price for our sins by the death of his only son. Thereby God forgives us of our sins, and opens up to us the prize of eternal life.

But even a cursory review of the dynamics of creation and a short review of human history, even through a biblical lens, reveals the presence of evil and the ubiquity of suffering and death that cannot only be sourced by human action and decision. There is cosmological expression of evil and destruction throughout the universe. There is natural suffering and death woven through the dynamics of the cycles of all life and death. And there are events in human history and in individual human lives that God freely admits to being the author.

The omnipotent and omniscient creator of all that is and all ever comes into being is responsible for the daily suffering and death that marks the lives of all people. Whether God actually caused suffering and death in human life, like in natural disasters, floods, diseases, calamities, or whether God simply permitted the sinful circumstances of humanly caused suffering and death, God is responsible. No theory of theodicy can ever avoid this basic truth.

The goodness of God only emerges as God's willingness to repent: "And the LORD changed his mind about the disaster (evil) that he planned to bring on his people" (Exodus 32:14, NRSV), and God's resolve to pay for the sins brought upon God's people. For God so loved the world that God sacrificed his own being so that humankind would not die, as he originally intended, but would live, and live forever. (John 3:16) Jesus died to pay for God's sins, to repent of the suffering and death brought about by God, so that in the end we would live free of suffering and death.

Corazon Puro

In the fall of 2014, Marsha and I decided that in the spring the following year we would walk the Camino de Santiago, the five-hundred mile walk across the countryside of northern Spain. The Camino is a pilgrimage walk undertaken by the faithful in search of the holiness of God which culminates at the Cathedral of Santiago de Compostela where tradition holds that the bones of St. James the Apostle are buried. Pilgrims have untaken the journey for almost 1,000 years, coming from all around the world.

For many the pilgrimage is conceived of as a spiritual journey, a quest for spiritual growth, testing or retreating from the pressures of busy modern life. The pilgrimage is also conceived of as commemorating and memorializing the loss of a dear loved one or respected spiritual leader. Marsha and I clearly dedicated our pilgrimage to the memory of our grandson, C.C. Our pilgrimage was to be a way to remember, celebrate and give thanks for C.C. He would be present with us in our hearts every step of the way in our pilgrim journey.

The 500-mile walk would be challenging physically, emotionally and spiritually. We began preparing for the journey right away. We began taking regular walks and hikes around our home and in Maryland. We challenged ourselves to go greater distances each day, knowing that the Camino would require walking up to 15-20 miles every day. We tried to prepared ourselves mentally for less dependance on modern technology, living simply, and disciplined eating.

But the preparation itself brought new physical and emotional challenges. On an early hike in the woods near our home, I slipped sown a muddy slope and tore a ligament in the meniscus of my knee. It required treatment but thankfully no surgery. But still it caused pain and discomfort, casting doubt on my ability to walk long distances. Two members of my extended family died in the fall and winter of that year, requiring travel and funerals. My perennial issues with longstanding health arose: my lower back pain and inflammation returned with a vengeance, and my chronic bronchitis returned for a month or two of coughing.

And then just shortly before we were scheduled to leave for Spain to begin the Camino, I was diagnosed with prostate cancer. I had to research my treatment alternatives while preparing to leave.

After deciding that surgery was my best course of action, I had to determine whether it was wise to proceed with the surgery and cancel the Camino, or to postpone the surgery until mid-summer upon my return from Spain. With some trepidation and uncertainty, I decided to postpone the surgery. As it turns out, that was probably not the wisest decision after all.

We left for Spain in early May planning to begin the Camino on the 14th of the month. Arriving in Madrid proved to be a daunting, complicated, and frustrating ordeal. Transfer from the international airport to the train station to travel in country involved finding and boarding a shuttle train. Unfortunately, Marsha left her waist pack which contained her wallet, IDs, credit cards and cell phone on the shuttle. We tried to file a lost and found claim at the train station but we soon realized there was no hope of finding and returning our valuables.

On the train taking us up north to Pamplona, we began the process of cancelling credit cards, restoring IDs, and turning off the cell phone. In a moving train with scanty cell service and spotty Wi-Fi access this was a very frustrating process. A heavy rain began falling across all northern Spain.

We arrived in Pamplona and found our local transportation to the first house of hospitality on the Camino. The house was located about halfway up into the Pyrenes mountains, close the official starting point of the Camino Frances, the route that begins at the southwestern French border. The house was called "Corazon Puro", which translates as "pure heart." At that point in our Camino pilgrimage, I was feeling anything but a "pure heart." In fact, as we sat down for a lovely dinner at Corazon Puro, I began to be overcome with a deep sense of panic and anxiety.

All the pressures, stresses and worries that had accumulated in the preparation and travel to Spain, the profound existential shock of the cancer diagnosis, and then the deep sense of fear and anxiety of walking the long miles across Spain, combined to send me reeling into a whirlwind of panic and depression. But most presciently the bottomless pit of grief that filled my broken heart from the death of our beloved grandson, C. C., made it impossible for me to contemplate taking just one step on the long pilgrimage to memorialize and celebrate his life. I just wasn't ready to do this.

I stayed awake all night that first night in Corazon Puro, body shaking, chills and sweat, visions of rain-soaked muddy paths, grueling long distances through cities and country-sides. By morning it was clear that I could not do the Camino. I had failed the first test of the pilgrimage. I could not take even the first step. In truth and all honesty, I was broken. I was lost. There was no way to find my way home.

That morning we turned away from Corazon Puro. Marsha was not ready to give up. She was not crippled by the same anxiety as me, but she was willing to give up the Camino for me. She loved me, supported me and counseled me through this crisis of faith. We went back to Pamplona, stayed a few days and then made our way back to Madrid. Shortly thereafter we were able to get a flight back home.

I was able to schedule prostate surgery for two weeks later. I spent the rest of my three-month sabbatical resting and recovering, and trying somehow to make sense of the battle with darkness that I had over taken my life and my ministry. I reviewed everything that had happened in the six months prior to beginning the Camino. I relived the last days of the trip to Spain, the struggle in the Madrid airport, the transfer in Pamplona. I tasted the soup and bread that we ate in the last supper at Corazon Puro, and I recreated the fitful visions of that long night afterward.

But ultimately, I had to review my whole life. I had to revisit the first whisperings of my call to ministry, the first stirring of God in my childhood, the first venturing into speaking of God in college, the first fitting of the robe of ministry in seminary, the first sermons from the pulpit, and the first prayers in dialogue with the divine. I recalled every act of ministry that had filled over forty-five years. This was not a quick process. I spent the next three years in counseling and spiritual direction trying to make sense of my dark night of the soul.

Finally, I came to understand that Corazon Puro was my last day in ministry. That lonely night in the deep countryside in Spain would be the last night real ministry within me. I had spent most of my life, giving witness to the ubiquity of human suffering and the testifying to the power of love to conquer the universality of death. Every sermon, every prayer, every song, every act, every embrace, was meant to share the love of God for every human being.

Something stopped that rainy night, and would never resume again. I did return from my sabbatical however. I preached many more sermons, spoke many more prayers. I performed many more funerals and memorial services. I spoke as more bodies were lowered into graves. But somehow, each of these were just a repeat, a recapitulation of the all the sermons and prayers said before. I had nothing new to bring to my ministry. My work was done. My ministry was complete.

12

POSTSCRIPT

I FIRST RECOGNIZED THE CALL to ministry late one night, as I walked across the campus of Southern Baptist Theological Seminary in Louisville, Kentucky. Looking into the cold clear night, stars shining brightly overhead, cold fall wind blowing across my face, I was overwhelmed with the conviction that I had been given an undeniable and irrevocable task to do for God. God was calling me to service with all of my being and all of my strength. God had something for me to do.

Earlier that evening I had attended a special showing of a movie, *The Last Nuclear War*. It was presented by the local chapter of a national anti-nuclear weapons organization. The movie was not a Hollywood production, but was an imagined documentary of what a potential nuclear war would be like. The movie created a scenario of rising tensions between the US and the Soviet Union, culminating in a pre-emptive nuclear strike against somewhere in the heartland of the United States.

The film depicted a creation of an actual nuclear explosion as it devastated a huge area of the country. The film showed the area affected by just one of the nuclear devises, hundreds of miles in circumference. Then it showed the effect of a thermo-nuclear explosion on buildings, houses and commercial structures, total devastation, total destruction.

Then the film showed the effects on human beings. It graphically showed how hundreds of thousands of people would be virtually incinerated in a matter of seconds. And then it made clear that in such a nuclear attack it would not be just one nuclear explosion, but thousands. The US and the Soviet Union had at that time over fifty-thousand nuclear warheads in their arsenals and the scenes depicted in this movie would be repeated thousands of times.

It became very clear to me that night, that God was calling me to a ministry that was focused very specifically on preventing the outbreak of nuclear war, of working for the complete disarmament of all nuclear weapons, and resolving the differences between the super powers of the world peacefully without war. That calling gradually became more generalized to become work for the peaceful resolution of all conflicts and the establishment of just relationships between all peoples. The call became the work for world peace and justice for all nations.

My seminary education was re-located to prepare for this refocused calling. I transferred to Union Seminary in New York City which was already deeply involved with liberation theology and justice ministries. My seminary internships were with the United Nations, and I balanced my classroom time with activist involvement with local and national peace and justice organizations. I became a minister organizer in the religious community long before I was ordained to be a minister in the church.

I organized rallies, demonstrations, teach-ins and educational events, even a certain amount of actual lobbying with government leaders. After my calling shifted again to be located in the local congregation, I still conceived of that pastoral ministry to be shaped by the work of justice and compassion.

The first congregation I served, Clifton Presbyterian Church, was deeply committed to ministry in the homeless community. Clifton Church ran a shelter for 30 homeless men, open 365 days a year, who slept on the floor of the sanctuary, the same space where worship happened on Sunday. Clifton was also a sanctuary church for Central American refugees, and a More Light Congregation for LGBT Christians.

The second congregation I served, Silver Spring Presbyterian Church, was also a More Light Congregation, and the majority of its members were immigrants from Africa. Many of the immigrants were refugees seeking a new life of freedom and safety. The ministry at Silver Spring was always based in justice and compassion.

After I retired from pastoral ministry I began to reflect on the course, direction and purpose of that ordained ministry over forty years, indeed a whole life of calling by God, and I began to change my understanding of it all. I reviewed my first memory of a conscious relationship with God, of God's deep presence and power in my life. I remembered every movement in my life in response to that presence and power. I brought to mind every experience of prayer and purposeful struggle with the word of God in my heart. I remembered every word and action that could be specifically associated with ministry in God's name—every sermon, every prayer, every song of praise and lamentation, every work of compassion and service.

After it was all put together, I realized something. My ministry was not about peace and justice organizing. It was not about changing hearts and minds and making the world a better place. It was not about changing the institutions and structures of the world or changing the lives of individual people to bring peace and harmony with God.

No, the real purpose and direction of my ministry was this: everything I said and did, every prayer and sermon, every work and mission was to give witness to the all-pervasive suffering of humanity, individuals and societies, and to testify to the presence and participation of God in midst of that suffering and the inevitable conclusion of death.

It began as I walked down the aisle of my Baptist church when I was seven years old in response to the suffering and dying of Jesus on the cross. It grew as I stood next to the dead body of my grandfather at 17. It became crystal clear as I stood on the mountain peak in Canada while hitching across the country in 1972. It became overwhelming as I discovered the murder of millions of Jews, gays, disabled and Roma people during the Holocaust of World War II.

My heart was broken forever as I stood next to the suffering of my grandmother, burned beyond recognition, abandoned by God. I was powerfully stirred to action by the visage of potentially millions incinerated in a nuclear war, and later weeping at the reality of the state incinerating an incarcerated man in the electric chair in Georgia.

My ministry was quickened by the companionship with homeless men walking the streets of Atlanta, while that same ministerial presence was softened touching the head of a week-old prematurely born infant as he lay dying in an incubator. I sang songs of God's praise and glory holding the hand of a seminary professor as she lay dying of cancer, and preached a sermon celebrating and giving thanks for the life of a homeless man who had died on the street alone.

I kissed the brow of my mother slowly dying from a broken heart and a broken body. I held the hand of my father delirious with visions of horror as he lay dying alone in a hospital bed.

I read poetry with the spiritual leader of the congregation as she lay long days in her bed, month after month, body undermined by pancreatic cancer, before, one day, she just closed her eyes for the last time.

I prayed next to the body of a new immigrant from Cameroon who had been murdered by the police in Montgomery County, Maryland. I sang a chorus of "Bend Low and see what the Lord do," next to a great saint of the church as she succumbed to the ravages of a stroke. I performed the funeral for a young woman whose body was riddled by cancer, while her infant son was being held by her mother, herself grieving the loss of her husband just months before.

As I bent over to hug the weakened body of a brilliant psychoanalyst and beautiful singer, he stretched up and kissed me on the cheek. He slipped away just a week later.

I futilely tried to comfort a young father whose wife and three young children were consumed in a house fire. How can that be done? I stood next to the body of my dead grandson, without a word, lost in steel-eyed horror and grief.

And through it all, from beginning to end, in every word and prayer, in every song and silence, I gave witness to the universal suffering of God in the life, death and resurrection of Jesus Christ. Emmanuel, God with us and for us. My work is done. My ministry is complete.

About the Author

CURRIE BURRIS IS A RETIRED MINISTER in the Presbyterian Church (USA). He served as pastor for 18 years at Silver Spring Presbyterian Church in Silver Spring Maryland, and as pastor for 10 years at Clifton Presbyterian Church in Atlanta, Georgia. In over 44 years of ordained ministry, Currie's experience has combined a commitment to work for peace, justice and human rights, service to the church, and spiritual formation. He has worked in ministries with homeless people, refugees and new immigrants, as well as in multiracial/multicultural church contexts.

Rev. Burris has a Doctor of Ministry in "Spirituality and the Suffering of God" from Wesley Theological Seminary in Washington D.C., and Master of Divinity from Union Theological Seminary in New York City. He has travelled and served the church in Cameroon, Zimbabwe and Kenya. He is married with children, grandchildren, and plays the piano, guitar and hammer dulcimer.

ALSO BY CURRIE BURRIS

Burris, Currie. (2017) *All Things New: Sermons by Currie Burris.* Cleveland, Tennessee: Parson's Porch and Book Publishing